Accepting and ministering ... important to today's church. ... pastor and congregation who are serious about ministering to those touched by disabilities, but to every person in need. It is a wonderful resource.

—Buck Buchanan, First Evangelical
Free Church of Fullerton

Stan Carder writes as he ministers: with a heart full of zeal and tender compassion for the needs of the disabled. I know of no one anywhere who is more gifted or better equipped to write a book such as this. I'm very grateful to see it in print, and my prayer is that it will be widely used to fortify and multiply ministries to the disabled in churches around the world.

—John F. MacArthur Jr., Grace Community Church

Pastor Stan Carder is no armchair theologian. Biblical truth and down-to-earth church life compassionately come together in this "must reading" which has been painfully, but patiently, hammered out on the anvil of firsthand experience. I wholeheartedly commend *A Committed Mercy*.

—Richard Mayhue, Senior Vice President and Dean,
The Master's Seminary

A Committed Mercy is a strategic and timely statement. It will be a welcome resource to caregivers as they minister to the many who are dealing with the really tough struggles of life.

—Joseph M. Stowell, President, Moody Bible Institute

When an author has *lived* a ministry in his home and has *expanded* it through his church, you can be sure he knows what he's writing about. This is a practical primer about a vital ministry, and it should be read by every Christian who wants to serve more like Jesus.

—Warren W. Wiersbe, Distinguished Professor of
Preaching, Grand Rapids Baptist Seminary

Why do we so often overlook those who need us most? Jesus didn't, nor should we. Stan Carder, from experience and from his heart, gives us courage and tools to do what all of us know we need to do—minister effectively to the disabled.

—H. B. London Jr., Vice President, Ministry Outreach/
Pastoral Ministries, Focus on the Family

A COMMITTED MERCY

You and Your Church Can Serve the Disabled

STAN CARDER

FOREWORD BY JONI EARECKSON TADA

Baker Books

A Division of Baker Book House Co
Grand Rapids, Michigan 49516

Published by Baker Books
a division of Baker Book House Company
P.O. Box 6287, Grand Rapids, MI 49516-6287

Printed in the United States of America

Library of Congress Cataloging-in-Publication Data

Carder, Stan, 1949–
    A committed mercy : you and your church can serve the disabled / Stan Carder ; foreword by Joni Eareckson Tada.
        p. cm.
    ISBN 0-8010-9004-0 (paper)
    1. Pastoral care of the handicapped. I. Title.
    BV4335.C35 1995
    259'.4—dc20   95–15372

Scripture quotations identified KJV are from the King James Version of the Bible.

Scripture quotations identified NASB are from the New American Standard Bible, © the Lockman Foundation 1960, 1962, 1963, 1968, 1971, 1972, 1973, 1975, 1977.

Scripture quotations identified RSV are from the Revised Standard Version of the Bible, copyright 1946, 1952, 1971, and 1973 by the Division of Christian Education of the National Council of the Churches of Christ in the United States of America.

This book is dedicated to:

My wife, **Ruth**, whose support, faithfulness, and sacrificial love are so beautifully modeled in the statement, "She is velvet-covered steel!" Proverbs 31 is alive and well in my wife of over twenty years. I am a grateful husband.

My son, **Jeremy**, a godly young man whose time and tenderness were given to me during my recuperation and continue to be given to all to this day.

My daughter, **Kim**, whose patience and wisdom with the disabled is beyond her years, yet fresh enough to minister with sensitivity to the smallest need at any time or in any situation.

My son, **Jason**, without whom our lives would have never been complete and who has changed us to be more like our Savior. His ministry in our lives and to those around the world is not because of his disability but because of his ability being molded by God into his character and likeness.

CONTENTS

FOREWORD

I'm thrilled that Baker Book House is publishing Stan Carder's book on pastors' involvement in disability ministry. It's needed. At JAF Ministries, we receive thousands of letters, many from family members of disabled individuals, but many more from pastors.

These pastors are often looking for "a place to start" because a family member in their congregation has sustained an injury, received a diagnosis of a disease, or, perhaps, given birth to a handicapped child. I'm struck by the fact that these pastors want very much to help, but they have no idea where to begin.

What I appreciate about Stan's book is that he has written it for the pastor of the small church—the church that often does not have the resources to develop an extensive disability outreach. These are the churches that are simply scrambling to meet the pressing needs of their own church families, and invariably some of those families include a member with a handicapping condition.

A Committed Mercy is needed. Pastors will be encouraged; churches will be strengthened; and most of all, families of disabled persons will be touched for Christ.

Joni Eareckson Tada

Acknowledgments

Thanks to Dorothy Clark for the excellent material she has developed to make congregations more aware of their need to minister to the disabled.

Thanks to Gene Neuman for his fine expertise in the area of child learning theory. His knowledge of mental retardation is vast, and his wisdom in teaching is much admired.

Thanks to Joyce Modert for her strong commitment to this book in both moral support and secretarial skills. Without her help, my ideas would have never seen the printed page.

Thanks to Susan Layton for her great patience in deciphering my handwriting. Her patience and secretarial skills in the polishing process have helped reflect the intent of this book.

Thanks to the faithfully committed staff of workers in special ministries at Grace Community Church. The past ten years have been wonderful. Your lives of sacrificial service will be placed alongside those saints in Thessalonica as you have truly modeled to the disabled and to myself the truths of 1 Thessalonians 2:20, "For you are our glory and joy."

INTRODUCTION

"Susan, did we contact Jeff about communion on Sunday night?"

"No, I'll do that right away. By the way, what are your sermon titles for Sunday? It's Thursday and I've got to finish the bulletin by tomorrow night."

Man, I've hardly had time to study, much less think of a title. This is crazy. I thought I'd have a lot more time when I got out of seminary!

"Is Mrs. Johnson still in Mercy General Hospital or did she go home? A family asked about taking a meal over to her." *I should have visited her more often. She is so old and frail. With her husband gone and her family so far away, we really need to have the congregation look after her. I know they care, but . . .*

"I don't know for sure, Pastor, but I'll find out right away. Which family wants to take the food? I'll contact them for you."

What a blessing a faithful secretary is.

"Pastor, you need to take this call now. It's Mrs. Jones. She's crying and she's very upset. Her daughter has just given birth to a baby with Down's syndrome. She's on line 2."

What am I going to say? I never had a class in seminary that dealt with this type of circumstance! I don't even have a book I can use to help me read up on this situation! Lord, help me say that right thing! "Hello, Mrs. Jones. This is the pastor. How are you doing?" *O Lord, help me . . .*

Lord, you have given me such a wonderful flock. It's such a privilege for me to be their under-shepherd. Harriet's such a faithful teacher. Lord, bless her. There's Rich. He has served our disabled so faithfully. Lord, he looks terrible! I wonder what's wrong.

"Hey, Rich, how's it going?"

"Pastor, I'm so concerned. We've worked so hard with Tommy, and he just doesn't seem to be making any progress spiritually. I never know if he is understanding the Bible lessons. All he wants to do is doodle and draw pictures. I'm so frustrated, I'm ready to quit!"

This office scenario is repeated daily across our land involving pastors of all types of congregations and of all denominations. Faced with this kind of phone call, the pastor often pushes the mental panic button and engages his mouth in conversation before he has quieted his heart in prayer.

Unexpected phone calls—no one likes them, but everyone has been annoyed or surprised by them. They have a history of coming at the most inopportune times—when you're enjoying a wonderful dinner your wife has fixed for that special occasion, or you've planned a great evening at home with the family, or maybe you're in a deep sleep that your body and mind have needed for a long time.

Those unexpected phone calls also have a history of changing lives forever. What emotion a parent feels when the phone rings and the son announces that there is going to be a family wedding and you're going to have new in-laws! Your mind races with questions: Is he really old enough? She's a wonderful girl, but is she ready to be a wife? She's so young (Weren't we all!). Or that unexpected phone call letting you know that you're new grandparents. You knew the baby was coming, but you just weren't certain when the grand event would happen.

Unexpected phone calls—what pleasure they bring! But not all calls have such a joyous ending. Our heads whirl when we receive information that a close friend or relative has just died. We know that death is inevitable; however, we are never prepared emotionally when the Grim Reaper has cut his path to our doorway. We are caught off guard; we don't know what to say, what to do, how to respond.

What do I say to those grief-stricken parents who have just found out that their daughter will be brain damaged due to an accident? What do I do for a new mother and dad whose world has been shattered when they have just discovered that their firstborn child is physically disfigured? The delight of anticipation has now turned into dread. The singing has turned into sobbing. Tears of joy have changed to tears of pain and anguish. Are there any words of comfort or deeds of kindness that can show the depth of my concern?

It is interesting that in medical emergencies the Christian community is often quick to respond. We stop by the house to drop off casseroles, and we send cards and offer our condolences. And yet as the emergency enters into a crisis of a few days, or even weeks, there seem to be fewer and fewer words of encouragement and deeds of kindness. After the crisis has dissipated and the day-by-day trial of caring for and nurturing the suffering person begins, the body of Christ is often negligent in its support to the family member and the family peers. As the magnitude of the tragedy begins to unfold, at the time of greatest need, the church so often is the least supportive!

People are busy; life is hurried with all its demands and activities. Yet for some families, time has stopped. The routine of waking up, maintaining the bedside vigil at the hospital or home, fixing a quick sandwich, and falling into bed utterly exhausted will be repeated for days, weeks, months, and maybe even years. This is not just an opportunity for the church to exercise its support for the family who suffers; this is a mandate to be fulfilled as the commandments to the "one anothers" in Scripture are obeyed and fleshed out in the lives of fellow believers. Scripture says we are to love, pray, encourage, and bear one another's burdens.

The first part of this book, chapters 1 through 3, is designed to assist the pastor in working with the congregation to accept all individuals whether disabled or able-bodied. At the end of each of the chapters are questions that are designed to probe, challenge, and develop your thinking into a biblical framework for effective ministry to those with disabilities. The charts in this section are designed to enhance your understanding of a family's mind-set when suffering and crisis are encountered.

The second part of this book, chapters 4 through 8, is designed to assist the teacher in motivating the handicapped student not only to understand his or her faith but to grow and mature to be more Christlike in everyday living. It is not a question of whether the disabled *will* learn, but rather a question of effectiveness in the teaching technique. It is not *can* they learn, but rather *how* they learn.

Since the learning environment enhances the truth being taught, it is imperative that every worker in special ministries understand the concepts on these pages and remain vigilant in pursuing biblical truth with excellence in every area of the student's learning experience.

The material in this book is not designed just to increase your knowledge about ministering to families and individuals whose lives are touched by disability, but rather to be utilized by you as a member of the body of Christ to reach out and minister to all who are in need. The question is not *if* you will use this material, but *when* you will use it. Are you prepared to minister? Are you equipped to minister?

Excuse me. The phone is ringing.

1

ONCE UPON A TIME

Bad Things Do Happen to God's People

The sun rose warm and bright over the Beartooth Mountains in Big Sky Country on June 29, 1981. Yet three hours later the beautiful day would be darkened in despair as oppressive clouds of death hovered above my newborn child. Born with Down's syndrome, our child had a life-threatening birth defect that was quickly taking his life minute by minute. As the doctor explained the danger of the moment and the necessity of emergency surgery in order to save his life, my mind entered the dreamland of denial and rejected the reality of the situation. I was painfully brought back to the truth as my wife and I cradled this precious life in our arms. With a prayer of dedication given by the doctor and each of us as his parents, we yielded him into the arms of God for his safe arrival to a hospital five hundred miles away. Hurried phone calls and emergency arrangements for my other two children were completed, and I boarded a small plane with my wife only three hours after delivery in order to be with our son at Primary Children's Hospital in Salt Lake City.

As we entered a new world of childhood suffering, little did we realize that our lives would never be the same. Scrubbing down before we could touch our son, we glanced into the ICU room filled with critically ill and dying newborns who were connected to every imaginable medical apparatus designed to assist them in their fight for life. Our eyes fell on the incubator marked Jason Theodore Carder. We were stunned and overcome with emotion. This was our wonderful son. This was our precious son. This was our dying son. What anguish of heart!

In the midst of our sorrow, a godly man who would be instrumental in saving our son's life and healing our turbulent emotions entered into our lives. With a "Jesus First" pin on his lapel and his incredible medical knowledge and expertise, Dr. Michael Matlack, our pediatric surgeon, tenderly explained all that would be necessary in order to save our son. We entrusted our son into his hands, beginning a routine in which, over the next eighteen months, this surgeon would rebuild Jason's intestinal tract so that he would enjoy a fruitful and joyous life.

During the time of the surgeries, the dream world of denial turned into the world of disillusionment and anger toward God. I was a pastor. I was continually ministering to the flock that God had entrusted to me. I was being faithful. Why me? Why now? Why this?

All the chains of doubt and despair that fettered my heart were broken one Sunday evening after I had spent the day ministering in the church. My wife began to minister to me by asking me some emotionally wrenching questions: "Do you love Jason?" and then, "Have you ever thanked God for Jason?" I knew I loved him, yet I wasn't sure that

I would or could ever be thankful for him. How could I be thankful for all of the pain and hurt that he had brought?

I realized then that being thankful was a choice, and that the emotions of acceptance and enjoyment of my child would only come after I was obedient to the command of 1 Thessalonians 5:18: "In every thing give thanks" (KJV). I realized that this verse was a command to be obeyed, not a thought to be pondered. When I prayed, "Lord make me willing to thank you for Jason," the chains of fear, doubt, worry, anger, and despair were broken, and my spirit was free!

Valuable lessons are often the hardest to learn. For sixteen months I had been a very poor student, but what a difference as we entered the hospital two months later for his last surgery and the reconnecting of the intestinal tract. Those long hours of waiting were rewarded with a complete success. No more colostomy problems! Now we had dirty diapers!

As the summer months approached, I was excited about my mini-vacation with Steve, a deacon in my church and a great employer. Even though the work of making concrete-poured walls was hard and tiring, it was a great way to supplement my small rural pastor's salary. As I was riding with Steve in the semi tractor trailer, it was refreshing to see a change of scenery. I also looked forward to visiting my parents in Kansas City.

After visiting my mom and dad for a few days, the truck was reloaded with new concrete wall forms, and we began to make our way back to Montana via Kansas, Colorado, and Wyoming.

After taking on 34,000 pounds of cargo and 80 gallons of fuel, we were ready to drive home. Steve was taking the first shift across the prairies of Kansas. Little did we know that in only fifty miles our truck-driving days would come to an end forever. Thirty minutes after we had started out, on June 2, 1983, at 6:00 P.M., the cargo and fuel were spilled across the Kansas Turnpike. Sound asleep in the sleeper unit, I had no knowledge of anything until I awoke upside down, wedged between the air conditioner and the seats. Trucks aren't designed to be comfortable, but that was ridiculous! After a few minutes and out of nowhere, I felt a hand on my leg and heard a man in a gray work uniform saying to me, "Son, don't move a muscle, and I mean don't move!" I never saw that man again. If I ever do find him, I would like to tell him that his advice saved my life. In the midst of my misery from six broken ribs and a damaged lung, I also had a broken neck. The upper part of the spinal cord controls many vital bodily functions, and the vertebrae that broke in my neck governed my breathing. Later the doctors confirmed that I had been only two pencil-lead widths from snapping the spinal cord, which would have caused instant death. To that man (an angel?) I owe my life.

As I lay in the hospital bed for those three weeks, I saw ministry take on a different dimension. It was the silent ministry that meant so much to my broken body—the cool washcloths on a body going into shock, the gentle holding of my hands as the pain ripped through my head when the bolts were screwed into my skull, the kind touches of a helping hand steadying my legs when I learned to walk again. Gentle words spoken in a soothing manner assured me that I would survive this ordeal. Silent ministry. Unheralded heroes and heroines quietly ministered without fanfare or spotlight. Often unnoticed by others, they were never forgotten by myself or our Lord.

During the many months of my recovery, we were asked to become involved in the special ministries program of Grace Community Church. I had no background in the field of special education other than experience, but the staff of the church felt that experience was the best training I could have. I have sought to be faithful to those disabled individuals that God has given me ever since then.

As I look back on the trials that God has brought across our path, the truth of Romans 8:28 has taken on a new perspective: "We know that all things work together for good" (KJV). That passage does not say that all things are good. It does not even say that all the bad things will become good. But it does say that all things will work together to produce the good. We live in such an instant society. Our microwave mentality has programmed the minds of believers to want an instant answer to why God allows certain things in our lives. We must learn to realize that in God's time and in God's mysterious ways, he will produce good out of difficult situations and broken bodies. The good that came from my experience is outlined in the chapters of this book.

REFLECTIONS

1. What experiences have you, your family, or someone close to you had with being disabled in some way?

2. Do you have any firsthand experience being in a hospital? What emotions did you feel while you were there?

2

But They're So Different

Ministering to the Disabled

Contrary to what many would and should expect, the church of Jesus Christ has not excelled in reaching the disabled. Transportation to attend church and Bible studies is often not available. Very few churches have programs for the mentally handicapped, the deaf, or the physically disabled, and even fewer churches have programs well-founded on biblical principles using appropriate learning theories. It is not enough to have a heart filled with sympathy for the disabled; that sympathy must be translated into action. This is the essence of true, biblical compassion.

A glimpse through the Gospels will overwhelm the casual reader with the extent of Christ's ministry to those who were lame, blind, or disabled in other ways. Over and over, the heart of Christ was moved with compassion because the people were like sheep without a shepherd. What was true two thousand years ago is tragically true today. There are so few "shepherds" for the disabled today.

The disabled do not want our pity; they want our commitment. We should never look at disabled people as problems within our world, but rather as people who *have* problems. Looking to Jesus Christ as our example, we never see him simply ignoring the plight of the people around him. Instead, he is seen translating that emotion of compassion into action to help those in need. Matthew 9:36 shows Jesus moved with compassion. In the next verses he tells his followers to beseech the Lord to send laborers to meet the needs of the bewildered sheep.

As we examine the church today, we must ask ourselves why the church has been so slow to return to Christ's model of ministry to the disabled. Here are at least three underlying reasons:

- *Lack of awareness.* The Christian community is not aware of the prevalence of handicapping conditions within our society. One out of seven individuals is handicapped. More than forty-two million Americans have a disability.
- *Fear.* Handicapped individuals represent an unknown, and people are afraid of the unknown. This book will help you overcome your fear by exposing you to the characteristics and needs of the disabled.
- *Lack of knowledge.* Most individuals in the church lack the necessary knowledge and training required to work with the handicapped. As a result, people use this as an excuse not to minister to this neglected segment of the church population.

As a result of this reasoning, one of the blights against the evangelical church of this century has been its treatment of the disabled. Often because of poor theology or the archaic view that disabilities were the result of sinful actions and attitudes, the church has been woefully inadequate in fulfilling its duty to evangelize and disciple disabled individuals. The question, Why bother? has sounded far too often from the lips of Bible-believing pastors. Yet as we view the pages of Scripture, we see that by his example, Jesus was constantly affirming the value and dignity of the disabled. If the evangelical church is to be Christlike in its actions and attitudes, it must adopt Christ's model of affirming all individuals regardless of physical or mental limitations.

> Changing our attitudes, or the attitudes of others, is not easy. We are trying to follow Jesus Christ, but we live in communities and tend to reflect the cultural attitudes of those communities. Social distinctions often are based upon physical attraction. Because a person looks different, we assume that one is different in all ways and tend to set such a person apart from the group. It is not easy to change these learned ways of feeling and reacting. But change we must. Though rejection is not a new experience for most persons with disabilities, rejection at church is especially inappropriate because inclusive love and concern should characterize the Christian fellowship.[1]

Once the congregation realizes that inadequate affirmation has taken place, a remedy must be sought and a process developed that will change the mind-set of the congregation. The concept of "like shepherd, like sheep" occurs frequently throughout the New Testament. In various passages Paul states the importance of imitating his personality and lifestyle as he imitates the life of our Lord (1 Thess. 1:6). So it is within the congregation; people will model what has been shown by their pastor. A pastor should model the attitudes shown by our Lord in the following story.

It happened twelve years ago. The small problem had turned into the ravaging disease of internal hemorrhaging that was slowly destroying her vitality. After rushing from one doctor to the next, taking one prescription after another, and spending the little she had saved, she was left in a state of physical weakness, emotional despair, and financial ruin. Hope was gone, money had vanished, and friends had mysteriously faded away in the time of her greatest need. Sound familiar? It seems as if it should be in the *Los Angeles Times* or the *Daily News*, yet the story is told in Mark 5.

It is interesting that in this story Jesus had just been approached in another crisis situation. Jairus's daughter had just died, and the panic-stricken father was pleading with Jesus to restore her to life. Though the crowds were squeezing him, and though his ear was attentive to the pleading cry of a father on behalf of his daughter, the Master's heart heard the desperate heart-cry of a woman unwanted and unneeded by society. In the midst of the crowds, he sought the individual. In the midst of the hustle and bustle of life, he took the time to minister tenderly to the needs of a despairing woman.

As a student of the Word, the pastor has only to give a cursory examination of the Gospels to see that Christ was often directly involved in the lives of disabled individuals. Many were filled with diseases (Mark 5). Others were blind (John 9), deaf (Mark 7), or palsied (Mark 2); yet Christ never turned them away because of their inability to function according to the standards of society. So it should be in the twentieth century. Through preaching, personal involvement in friendships, and Christlike personality, the pastor should lead the congregation as an example of godly attitudes toward the disabled.

However, the disabled individual many times does not have the opportunity to personally interact with the pastor; therefore, it is imperative that the Spirit of God be allowed to work in the hearts of the congregation to break down attitudinal barriers toward the disabled. This breakthrough is seen in acceptance rather than avoidance. It looks past the problem that the person may have and sees the personality of the person that is confined within those physical or mental prisons. When pity is replaced by commitment, the able-bodied person is the one who receives the blessing of God and the benefit of greater relationship.

Robertson McQuilken, past president of Columbia Bible College, resigned his presidency because of the declining health of his wife, who was suffering from the ravages of advanced Alzheimer's disease. In his letter of resignation he wrote:

> My dear wife, Muriel, has been in failing mental health for about eight years. So far I have been able to carry both her ever-growing needs and my leadership responsibilities at CBC. But recently it has become apparent that Muriel is contented most of the time she is with me and almost none of the time I am away from her. It is not just "discontent." She is filled with fear—even terror—that she has lost me and always goes in search of me when I leave home. Then she may be full of anger when she cannot get to me. So it is clear to me that she needs me now, full-time.
>
> Perhaps it would help you to understand if I shared with you what I shared at the time of the announcement of my resignation in chapel. The decision was made, in a way, 42 years ago when I promised to care for Muriel "in sickness and in health . . . till death do us part." So, as I told the students and faculty, as a man of my word, integrity has something to do with it. But so does fairness. She has cared for me fully and sacrificially all these years; if I cared for her for the next 40 years I would not be out of debt. Duty, however, can be grim and stoic. But there is more; I love Muriel.

> She is a delight to me—her childlike dependence and con-
> fidence in me, her warm love, occasional flashes of that wit
> I used to relish so, her happy spirit and tough resilience in
> the face of her continual distressing frustration. I do not
> *have* to care for her, I *get* to! It is a high honor to care for
> so wonderful a person.[2]

What commitment! He had learned to look beyond the disability of his wife's problem and see the value and dignity
of the person. McQuilken faithfully ministers to his wife
because he sees her value. So must all believers, if the task
of ministering to the disabled is to be accomplished and
the task of the Great Commission is to be fulfilled.

However, mental battles war on the soul of the believer.
We are torn as we realize our God-given duty versus our
human emotion. The disabled often look funny. They may
act silly. They talk differently. They look, but often cannot see. They have ears, but they cannot hear. They are different. *Why bother?* Why should I minister to someone
who is so different from myself? Whether it is the foreign
mission field or the home field of forty-two million disabled Americans, the question, Why bother? must be answered from a biblical and God-honoring perspective.

In an age of instant everything and throwaway materials, it is tragic that society has often looked at the handicapped child as a disposable commodity. The recent court
cases regarding the right to life of the disabled fetus have
brought into serious question the value of the disabled person and have fostered debate on how human value is to be
determined. Many feel that value is based on how well an
individual functions—that is, his or her ability to experience thoughts and feelings and carry ideas into completed
action.

Billy was only two years of age when he was struck by
a raging infection that destroyed his brain. As the doctors
lifted the CAT scan pictures to the screen, my heart sank.

The images projected a brain that was virtually destroyed. Now blind, deaf, unable to speak, and unable to control his bodily functions, Billy has ministered to many people because they have realized that human value is based on a deeper foundation than body or brain function.

If ability to function is to be used as a standard, no one could measure up, because all of us have some type of impediment. Those with disabilities may be physically or mentally disabled, while the able-bodied may be disabled by hate, fear, anger, or other emotions. Another danger of using ability to function as the standard of viability is that other humans endow themselves with the right to determine who lives or dies. Who has the right to destroy the "Billys" of society? One man in World War II preached this concept and the world will forever hold him in contempt for practicing genocide on the European continent.

If fallible humans set themselves as the standard to determine life and death issues, three questions must be answered. First, what is the proper level of the standard of acceptance in order for life to be sustained? When is the ability to function reached? Second, who has the ultimate standard to determine who is functioning properly? Who is valuable? And third, who has the ultimate right to determine who is valuable? These questions raise an endless stream of questions that give rise to the danger of human speculation being used to determine issues that belong to God alone.

I would like to propose that a better way to answer the question, Why bother? would be that we seek to minister to the disabled because they are created in the image of God. As such they share with the Creator the attributes of God—characteristics such as love, mercy, power, and goodness. Furthermore, Christians should minister to the disabled because of our position as redeemed children of God.

Not only does our redemption motivate us to minister to the disabled, but we also have the example of Christ. In a careful examination of his life, we see our Lord ministering to people not out of pity, but out of true compassion. Pity is simply raw emotion, while compassion motivates us to action to see the situation change for the betterment of the person (Matt. 9:36–37; Mark 6). We may have an external motivation through community service, friends, or even a job, and we may have internal motivation through love for people or a desire to see better situations for others, but if we fail to have spiritual motivation (through obedience to Christ's example), we will quickly lose heart and experience emotional burnout.

Why bother ministering to those who have physical or mental limitations? I believe there are three basic reasons. First, we must model the life of Christ to others. His was one of compassion. Second, those who are different from us are also made in the image of God. Last, but certainly not least, we are all handicapped. Some may be more noticeably disabled than others, but no one is exempt.

Why bother? Since all of us are handicapped either emotionally, physically, or mentally, where would we be if Jesus had asked the very same question as he viewed his fallen creation on earth?

> Dear Pastor Brown,
>
> Just a quick note to you. I know that your schedule is swamped with so many other things, but I just wanted to drop you this line and let you know of a crucial decision that my husband and I have come to.
>
> After visiting your wonderful church and thoroughly enjoying your great messages, we have had to make the painful decision to leave your congregation. We want to assure you that it has nothing to do with you or your teaching. It has to do with our family.
>
> As you may have noticed, Larry and I have not been attending the services together. It is due to the fact that one of us has to stay at home and attend to the needs of our disabled child. You see, it is very difficult for Tommy to sit

still during your messages because of his limited capacity to comprehend your content due to his mental retardation. As a result he becomes restless and has a tendency to create quite a scene or commotion. Therefore, to avoid the stares, and out of respect for others' desire to worship, we thought it best to leave Tommy at home and one of us will be baby-sitting him here. Please pray for us. It is such a struggle to know how to best raise our son to be the young man that God desires.

Continue to preach your wonderful messages. Whenever we are able to hear them, they are always an encouragement and comfort to us.

Your Friends,
Larry & Sue

Tragically this letter could be duplicated over and over as it comes across the desks of a majority of the pastors in America. The frustration, isolation, and loneliness that such parents feel are caused by the fact that there is neither awareness of their need nor a program for their son to attend when they seek their own spiritual refreshment.

Overcoming Barriers

You may be saying, "I see the need, but how can I make myself and the congregation more aware of what needs to be done?" As a pastor, you may ask yourself, "Why won't the 'normal' people in our church get involved with our disabled?" The answer is simple—they are afraid of the disabled for a number of reasons, and, at the same time, they are afraid to admit that they are afraid. They may never open up and get involved unless you help them deal with their attitudinal barriers.

If a church does not have a well-planned congregational awareness program, chances are that everybody will miss out. The disabled will not experience the loving Christian fellowship and teaching that Jesus intends for his children, and the congregation will miss some rich blessings and valuable teaching that individuals with a disability have to offer (1 Cor. 12:7).

Following are some barriers that will need to be overcome in order to provide a proper congregational awareness of the disabled.

Attitudes

Attitudes and emotional responses often keep people from truly accepting the disabled person. People with disabilities are often referred to as "exceptional" individuals; however, they would much rather be "acceptable." Pastors and church members often approach a person with a disability in a condescending and patronizing manner rather than as a potential friend and associate. A person with a disability can easily sense the spirit in which a person is addressing him.

The person with a disability must not only cope with disability but must also deal with the responses of others. People in our culture strive to be associated with intelligent, successful, and healthy people. As a result of these attitudes, many people with an obvious disability have retreated to hide behind their handicap. Often, they find it too hard to face a society that rejects them.

Society, including Christ's church, is becoming more accessible and is opening its front doors to disabled people. However, these open doors are simply made of wood; the door to our hearts and lives often remains closed. One cannot expect people with a disability to be satisfied with a superficial love, a love that is spoken in word but lacks in deed.

Rarely do we fool people when we feel uneasy, unfriendly, or even alienated toward them. Attitudes toward the person with a disability often shut them out of the mainstream of life. Silence, stares, cold shoulders, and superficial smiles do not create an atmosphere of love and sharing or encourage worship of Jesus Christ our Lord.

Think back on your first encounter with a disabled person. How did you respond when a mentally handicapped person wanted to shake your hand or give you a hug? What were your emotions when a person with cerebral palsy sought to speak to you and was having great difficulty getting the words out? Were you embarrassed? Did you want to "hurry them up" to get the words out?

It must be remembered that people with disabilities have a special place in Jesus' heart, as seen in his ministry (Matt. 11:2–5). The church is contradicting itself by not actively accepting and gathering people with disabilities into its midst. Too often Christians let their attitudes dictate their level of acceptance of disabled people.

Emotions

Emotions may be described as our normal reactions and feelings in normal situations. They play a major role in the formation of our attitudes. They surge up within us in all kinds of situations, but especially toward people—love and hate, attraction and repulsion, fear and comfort, for example.

God created humans in his image. In doing so, God gave them expressive and emotional personalities like his own. God loves (John 3:16); God hates (Mal. 2:16); God gets angry (Exod. 4:14). Jesus was grieved and distressed (Matt. 26:37–38); and Jesus wept (John 11:33–35). God is perfect, and his emotional responses and attitudes are always justified. In contrast, since the fall, our sinful nature has created many painful and unjust attitudes about all aspects of life.

Emotions create our attitudes toward things, people, and all the circumstances of our lives. It must be remembered that emotions are natural; they are inborn characteristics that are intensified by knowledge and experience. Emotions are a result of one's past, present, and perceived future, and many times they govern our perspective of the past (events), present (happenings), and future (anticipation).

Emotional responses can be divided into two categories: positive and negative. Positive emotional responses have a constructive influence on oneself or others. In contrast, negative emotional responses have a destructive effect. These simplified definitions are open to criticism; nevertheless, it is the principle of differentiating between positive or negative emotional responses that is important at this point.

The following are steps we often use in expressing our emotions:

1. *Perceive.* You see a young boy sitting in a wheelchair with his head down.
2. *Feel.** You feel sorry for the sad, mentally retarded boy in the wheelchair.
3. *React.** You immediately look the other way for fear he will think you're staring, almost pretending he doesn't exist.
4. *Reason.* You may try to rationalize or even invent reasons for having reacted a certain way.
   *Reacting and feeling may take place at the same time or they may even be reversed from the order shown above.

The real situation: Johnny is ten years old and was born with cerebral palsy. He has a hard time holding his head upright due to his disability. He's sitting outside the game store because his mother could not carry him up the stairs. She's buying him a chess set because that's his favorite game. Johnny would most likely have loved meeting you and even talking about chess, which is your favorite game also.

Misconceptions

The last barrier that needs to be hurdled is misconceptions. People have created countless misconceptions about the disabled. As a result, the congregation may experience decreased performance, dampened reasoning ability, dulled creative thinking processes, discouraged relationships, distorted imagination, and destroyed peace and joy.

Misconceptions may also cause people to try to do too much or be oversolicitous in associating with a person with a disability. They may cause unwarranted sympathy, a sense of guilt, and a subconscious feeling of overresponsibility. We may try to do more than is actually reasonable for a person or more than is good for the individual. Misconceptions can create an insincere, smothering love that eventually does more harm than good. The following chart shows some of the major misconceptions in working with the disabled.

Major Misconceptions

Category	Description	The Truth
Failure	A handicap represents failure, and people are not good at living graciously with failures.	"And we know that God causes *all* things to work together for good to those who love God, to those who are called according to His purpose" (Rom. 8:28 NASB).
No Return	It's hard to give to people who have so little to give in return. It must be remembered, "No deposit, no return."	"But to each one is given the manifestation of the Spirit [spiritual gifts] for the common good [of the body of Christ]" (1 Cor. 12:7 NASB).

Life Changers	People like to see themselves as life changers, and if they help a handicapped person, he's still handicapped afterward.	"I came that they might have life, and might have it abundantly" (John 10:10 NASB).
Beautiful People	People like to be associated with intelligent, successful, beautiful people.	"Be of the same mind toward one another; do not be haughty in mind, but associate with the lowly. Do not be wise in your own estimation" (Rom. 12:16 NASB).

A major way that these misconceptions may be counteracted is by developing a good congregational awareness program. It should be:

- *Enriching.* It must first help members of the congregation develop a proper understanding of who they are in Jesus Christ (Eph. 2:10–11).
- *Experiential.* It must provide positive experiences and interaction with individuals who have a disability.
- *Informative.* It must present up-to-date facts about various disabling conditions and their effects upon an individual.
- *Correcting.* It must correct false information concerning handicapping conditions.

The process of applying these principles is practical and simple:

- The Bible is our basis (2 Tim. 3:16).
- Personal honesty is a must. A good place to start is for you to share some of the fears you had before you began working with these special people.
- Interest small groups. Begin with small groups within the congregation (e.g., Bible study groups or Sunday school classes). Allow these groups to plant seeds of interest in the rest of the congregation.
- Preparation and creativity are needed for a dynamic presentation.
- Personalized teaching will engage individuals.
- Move from simple and concrete. Teach from the known to the unknown (e.g., It is much easier for people to understand blindness than to come to grips with mental retardation).
- Teach in small doses. Give people a little at a time, just enough to whet their appetites so they will want to hear more.
- Have patience. Do not force people into getting involved. A premature involvement will cause people to pretend that everything is okay even if they may be questioning their willingness and ability to fulfill their teaching commitment.
- Ask for short time commitments. Do not ask people to make long-term time commitments at first.

As a result of these simple procedures, barriers will be broken down and friendships with the disabled established. The blessing of friendship is further extended within the body of Christ and true godly fellowship is fulfilled. This is seen in the following diagram.

Levels of Acquaintance

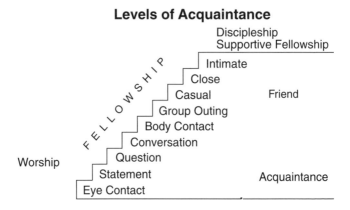

The diagram illustrates the various levels of acquaintance and friendship. Notice that as the level of friendship increases, the depth of fellowship is enhanced. Fellowship begins as two people attend the same church and worship the Lord Jesus Christ. This can grow into sharing prayer requests, Bible study, helping in times of crisis, and ultimately an intensive discipleship program and supportive fellowship.

Joe is a young man in my ministry whom I value as one of my dearest friends. Born with cerebral palsy, he is confined to a wheelchair. However, that is about all that confines Joe. His great sense of humor, infectious laugh, and great smile constantly draw me to him. As we have become more acquainted with each other, I never think about his body in a chair, but about a personality and spirit that are free in Christ. He faithfully teaches others, speaks and trains young children in the things of Christ, and ministers constantly to those who depend upon his prayers.

Connie, who suffers from multiple sclerosis, is bound in body but free in spirit. Her prayers, words of encouragement, and smiles of support have greatly enriched my life. Beginning with a nice introduction, this friendship has blossomed as it has been grounded upon our Lord and his Word.

These people don't need me but I have depended on their prayers and support so that the kingdom cause would go forward.

Is it worth it? How do I know if I can do it? What is the result of all my labor? How will I know if that mentally handicapped person will really understand me? Am I doing right as I help that physically handicapped person in the wheelchair? These questions can best be answered from the viewpoint of disabled persons themselves as expressed in the following anonymous writing.

Special Beatitudes

Blessed are you who take time to listen to difficult speech, *for* you help us to know that if we persevere, we can be understood.

Blessed are you who walk with us in public places and ignore the stares of strangers, *for* in your companionship we find havens of relaxation.

Blessed are you who never bid us to "hurry up"; and more blessed, you who do not snatch our tasks from our hands to do them for us, *for* often we need time rather than help.

Blessed are you who stand beside us as we enter new and untried ventures, *for* our failures will be outweighed by the times when we surprise ourselves and you.

Blessed are you who ask for our help, *for* our greatest need is to be needed.

Blessed are you who help us with the graciousness of Christ, *for* oftentimes we need the help we cannot ask for.

Blessed are you, when by all these things you assure us that the thing that makes us individuals is not in our peculiar muscles, nor in our wounded nervous systems, nor in our difficulties in learning, but in the God-given self that no infirmity can confine.

Rejoice and be exceedingly glad, and know that you give us reassurances that could never be spoken in words, *for* you deal with us as Christ dealt with all his children.

REFLECTIONS

1. What have been your personal attitudes toward the disabled?

2. As you think back over your childhood and youth, what was your first exposure to the disabled?

3. What was your initial reaction and response?

4. What steps have you taken to see that first response change into what it is today?

5. What course of action will you engage in that will see a change in the attitudes described previously?

3

WHY ME? WHY NOW? WHY THIS?

The Age-Old Question of Suffering

He could not sleep—he continually tossed until dawn.
He used dirt clods to cover his running sores.
Worms crawled in his flesh.
The thought of food made him sick.
His pain was so intense that he was forced to bite his
    own flesh to tear out the boils.
His flesh rotted before his very eyes.
The itching never ceased.
He was flushed and red from weeping.
His eyes were dark and recessed from lack of sleep.
His body was shriveled and wrinkled.
Job was exhausted and alone.
His breath was foul.
He could barely breathe.
His soul was bathed in bitterness.

He was emaciated to the point that his bones clung to
     his skin.
His flesh turned black.
He was constantly burning with fever.
And the pain never ceased.
The only place he could find to rest was in the ashes
     and dung and garbage outside the city among
          the beggars
               the outcasts
                    the lepers and
                         the dogs.
He was deserted by his friends and mocked by his
     enemies.
He describes himself as a rag doll, grabbed by the neck
     and shaken to pieces.
He was as a target set up and shot through with arrows.
His condition was so desperate,
     his appearance so contemptible,
          his pain so continual,
               his shame so complete,
     that his wife finally suggested that he kill himself.[3]

Suffering. The age-old question, Why do the righteous
suffer? is being asked hourly by God's children throughout the world. It seems that those who suffer can identify
with the sage of old—the man Job. During incredible suffering, Job asked some very important questions. Don
Baker in his excellent book, *Pain's Hidden Purpose*, states
it this way:

The Book of Job is not just a theological treatise:
     It does show God at His best, and
     it does show Satan at his worst.
     It is a revelation of God's sovereignty, and
     it is a revelation of man's helplessness.
     But . . . it is first and foremost

the story of a real man,
living in a real country,
suffering a real calamity.
It's the story of
one man's wealth
one man's family
one man's health
one man's reputation, and
one man's spirit
that is lost, destroyed, broken, and crushed beneath an intolerable load of pain and suffering.
It's the story of
one man's God
one man's faith
one man's enemy
one man's friends, and
one man's bewilderment,
as all the traditional values and traditional roles are thrown out of focus.

It's the story of a man who suffers without a cause and loses without a reason—and survives.

It's different from most personal tragedies, however. It's one of the few that tells the whole story, unlike an autobiography where a person tells his own story—as he sees it; or a biography, where a person tells another's story—as he sees it. This story adds another dimension. It's the story of a man's life as he saw it and as others saw it, but it's the story as Satan and God saw it also. It's the whole story.

It addresses the ofttimes unanswerables, like:
How did it happen?
and
Why did it happen?

It's one man's story, but it's every man's story, for in Job we have the "full picture" of calamity and suffering. And the "full picture" of Job's calamity and suffering is the "full picture" of your sufferings and mine.[4]

It is wonderful to know the outcome of the story of Job. It is not only a story of endurance, but also a story of hope—hope that even though the disabled suffer here, one day, because of the redemptive work of Christ on the cross and their accepting him as Lord and Savior, there will be deliverance and a new glorified body (1 Cor. 15). Pain and sorrow will be replaced with wholeness and joy. In the meantime, the pastor and the congregation should be involved not only in building bridges to and with the disabled, but also in counseling and assisting the disabled in their understanding of God's sovereign design for suffering.

Building a program is not the goal of ministry, but rather building people and restoring their brokenness. It is impossible to fully comprehend the infinite mind of God. We are limited by time and space, but the Almighty is limited only by what he chooses to limit himself with. Only through the redemptive process and the resulting renewing of our minds day by day can we attempt to understand the plans and purposes of God as revealed within his Word (Rom. 12:1–2). The Scriptures give the disabled the basis for comfort in the present and hope for the future. Utilizing the Scriptures accurately, the pastor and the congregation can assist the disabled in seeking answers to their questions on suffering. Passages such as Romans 8, 2 Corinthians 1, and Hebrews 4 give great comfort to those who are undergoing pain or times of trial.

George Peterson, in his book, *Helping Your Handicapped Child*, gives two very helpful charts to aid the pastor and the congregation in assisting the disabled to understand God's design for suffering.[5]

Origin and Value of Suffering

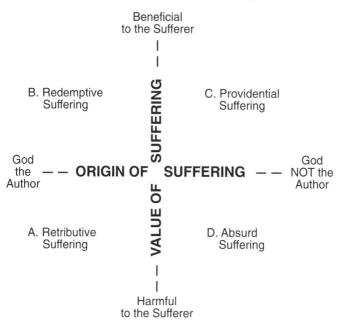

Attitudes toward Suffering

Redemptive Suffering
Acceptance
Cooperation
Gratitude

Providential Suffering
Faith
Patience
Hope

Retributive Suffering
Patient Submission

Absurd Suffering
Determined Resistance
Courageous Endurance

The determining factor in establishing a proper attitude is how the individual views the suffering.

No discussion of ministering to the disabled would be complete without mentioning the family. Individual disability is actually family disability, for the individual's pain and suffering is often reflected and expressed in the family. It is seen in relationships between husband and wife, between sibling and disabled child, and between family and community. All areas of social contact are significantly affected by the introduction of the disabled child into the family.

This was evidenced to us in a most personal way when we returned from Salt Lake City after our son with Down's syndrome had received life-saving surgery. We began to understand the impact that Jason would have on our family, friends, and congregation. Instead of "Congratulations!" "We're happy for you!" and "That's a good-looking baby," we were greeted with silence, avoidance, and stares. It was not that the people were being mean or insensitive; they simply didn't know how to respond or what to say. Such initial responses are not infrequent in local churches across America.

When the disabled child enters the family, through accident or birth, the family must work through the same stages of the grief process as if death had occurred. Although with a disability physical death has not taken place, there is a type of death that is very real, and that is the death of dreams. Every parent desires and expects to give birth to a child with no disabilities. Every parent seeks the safety and protection of the child. However, God may have other plans for that family. Either through birth or accident, glorious expectations and dreams become nightmares overnight. How parents handle the death of dreams will greatly affect the outcome of their emotional survival for future days. This is illustrated in the following chart.

God's Sovereign Design

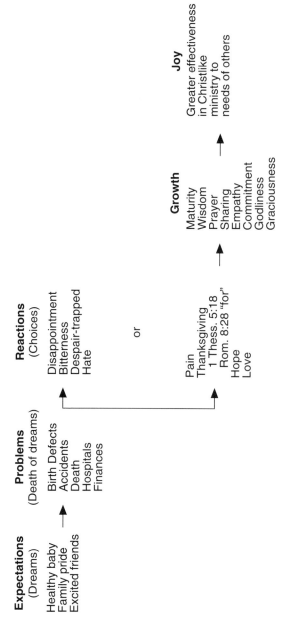

Expectations
(Dreams)

Healthy baby
Family pride
Excited friends

Problems
(Death of dreams)

Birth Defects
Accidents
Death
Hospitals
Finances

Reactions
(Choices)

Disappointment
Bitterness
Despair-trapped
Hate

or

Pain
Thanksgiving
1 Thess. 5:18
Rom. 8:28 "for"
Hope
Love

Growth

Maturity
Wisdom
Prayer
Sharing
Empathy
Commitment
Godliness
Graciousness

Joy

Greater effectiveness
in Christlike
ministry to
needs of others

Under the column entitled Reactions you will notice the word *choices.* The power of proper choice will determine the future emotions that the parents will live with as they deal with the death of their dreams. Included is the Scripture reference 1 Thessalonians 5:18, "In every thing give thanks" (KJV). Thankfulness for the mysterious dealings of God within the confines of one's life is not optional; it is essential. Feelings of joy and happiness are not conditional for thankfulness; they are the result of obedience to God's command of being thankful for all things. Notice that only an attitude of thankfulness will lead to growth and joy.

As we saw earlier, Romans 8:28 does not say that all things *are* good, or that all the bad things will eventually *become* good, but it does say that all things (good and bad) work together to *produce* good. The problem within our "instant" society is that we desire answers immediately instead of being able to wait to see what God's plan is for the situation that we are facing. One writer puts it this way:

> I asked God to take away my pride,
>   And God said, "No."
> He said it was not for Him to take away, but for me to give up.
>   I asked God to make my handicapped child whole,
>   And God said, "No."
> He said her spirit is whole, her body is only temporary.
>   I asked God to grant me patience,
>   And God said, "No."
> He said that patience is a by-product of tribulation, it isn't granted, it's earned.
>   I asked God to give me happiness,
>   And God said, "No."
> He said He gives blessings, happiness is up to me.
>   I asked God to spare me pain,
>   And God said, "No."

He said, "Suffering draws you apart from worldly cares
   and closer to Me."
   I asked God to make my spirit grow,
      And God said, "No."
He said I must grow on my own, but He will prune me
   to make me fruitful.
   I asked God if He loved me,
      And God said, "Yes."
He gave me His only Son who died for me, and I will
   be in heaven someday because I believe.
   I asked God to help me love others, as much as He
   loves me,
      And God said, "Ah, finally, you have the idea."[6]

Contrast the previous poem with the following letter
received by Triad Ministries of Denver, Colorado.

A Parent's Perspective

In the delivery room I held my baby close that rainy
night in July 1975. Nine months of growing eagerness sub-
merged quickly into icy fear. I saw her bluish pallor; I missed
her lusty newborn cry; I touched her little flat nose. I guessed
something was awfully, awfully wrong.

Within an hour the doctor confirmed my worst fears—
my daughter, the baby my husband and I had joyously
awaited, was a Down's syndrome child.

This could not be my child! I would not believe it. This
could not be the healthy baby of my dreams. This child in
my arms was retarded, and retardation did not fit my standards. Retardation to me meant less-than-human. But I was
not dreaming. I was awake. It was true. This baby was *my*
child!

Death would be better for her. Her death would erase my
pain—my pain for myself and my pain for her as a retarded
child. I felt totally separated from everyone, totally alone.
Was this really *my* child? Everyone, the staff, the minister,

my husband, and even I, spoke of "the baby," "her," and sometimes, "it." She was not a part of us; she was not a person. We talked of giving her up for adoption. We could not think of her as part of our family.

We named her Heather.

On that first awful day the doctor said he also suspected a heart defect. On that same day a colleague, a nurse, the mother of a Down's syndrome child, visited me. She said, "Your friends will accept your child the same way that you accept her." Nothing registered; I was too numb.

During the first two days our pastor spent time with us. It helped—a little. He promised to keep helping.

On the third day the doctor found that Heather had an intestinal obstruction; she would die shortly from starvation. Maybe that would be better, I thought dully. For Heather to live, he said, immediate surgery was required. "The decision," he said, "is yours."

What a decision! Death by starvation or a life of mental retardation! I did not want that decision. I could not make it. I could not take on the awful responsibility of allowing her to die. Guilt engulfed me. Yes, I had wanted her to die. But wouldn't death be better? Yet I was not God.

My husband also struggled painfully, but from a different viewpoint. He looked ahead; he saw a difficult future for a mentally retarded little girl, a difficult future for a husband and wife.

We needed spiritual guidance. But where was it? Our pastor had to leave town that third day. Our associate pastor was on vacation. We were worried, scared, and alone.

Our families urged us to go ahead with surgery. Wearily we let go. We signed papers. "It is in God's hands," we said. The heaviness of the responsibility for her life or death lifted very slightly, but the burden still overwhelmed us. "What do I pray for now?" I cried to myself. My question was left unanswered.

Surgery was successful and for three weeks Heather was in intensive care. Friends and church members strengthened and supported us. Their concern and care temporarily broke through the wall of hesitancy and fear of speaking openly about our retarded baby.

The retarded child we had brought into the world affected my husband and me differently as together and separately we worked through our grief. While I worried about Heather's physical problems, he worried about her retardation. When he worried about the future, I faltered under the present. Our inability to recognize each other's different worries led to misunderstanding, frustration, and anger. Later our pastor taught us the advantage of being at different levels of anxiety; we learned to support each other. Many times one of us could help the other through a particular pain by sharing our own handling of the pain.

When Heather was three weeks old she came home.

The first year was a kaleidoscope, a crazy blizzard of business and anxieties jostling chaotically in the confines of our small family. Thrice-weekly infant stimulation therapy crowded countless visits to doctors. Although insurance and state-funded therapy helped to relieve immediate financial disaster, we worried about our small savings and limited earnings as we faced the anxiety of possible heart surgery.

Progress was stilted, jerky. Each step of development brought hope, only to be dashed by the stop which followed as regularly as night follows day. What would heart surgery do to her or for her? New questions were raised about hearing loss. I wondered bitterly, "How many more things can they find wrong with her?"

Meanwhile, in the church many perfect babies were born. Part of me yearned to be included in the parental excitement, and part of me detested it. I was different; I was lonely; I was angry. Every get-together of young couples focused on sharing the accomplishments of their perfect babies. Accomplishments which always exceeded Heather's limited actions angered and depressed me.

I did not want to be excluded from conversations solely because my baby was different. Then I remembered my colleague's comment and tried to talk about Heather, brag about her accomplishments and express disappointment in her setbacks. I made a small beginning in accepting Heather as our real child, and friends watched me overcome my silent fear.

Yet, I could not fool myself. Our child was different, and like an evil leaven, a feeling permeated my being—we as parents were different too. We had to be different because we had produced a child who was different. Our interests and energies were different, not by choice but by necessity. While my friends were at home or on outings with their children, I was at therapy or sitting in doctors' offices. My friends discussed future financing of Christian education for their children, while I worried about financing heart surgery and therapy and worried about the possibility of any kind of education for my child.

The kaleidoscope of emotions in turmoil never settled; every moment of our lives and thoughts was affected by our different daughter. Nothing infuriated me so much as the smooth, "God must love you very much to entrust you with a child who requires so much special care." Some complimented me with, "You are an exceptional parent." My tired shoulders sagged and I compressed my lips to withhold an angry retort, both to God and to well-meaning friends.

My thoughts fought back: "I am no more well-equipped than you! I have no more wisdom than you! Courage? I have none; I am scared! Sure, it's easy for you to call me exceptional; it's easy for you to think God loves me so much. It takes you off the hook and you don't have to worry about me, because God will surely take care of the people he loves so much. But, don't you know that God uses people to carry out his love and support? Where are you when I need you?"

Separation and loneliness grew as my involvement in church decreased. Time was spent only with the family and a very few close friends. My anger at the pastors, the church, and Christians grew as the crises in our family continued, each with little, less, or no notice. Sure, people inquired graciously at church about Heather, but regular visits by pastors, elders, deacons, and church members stopped.

I cried inside for support from Christians, those who shared my spiritual and cultural background, but I had to seek my support from mothers of children like Heather. We mothers met weekly with social workers to vent our feelings and work through our problems. The state arranged and funded these meetings; the state understood my needs. Did the church care less than the state? How could I expect these mothers, whose religious backgrounds differed so from mine, to understand my response to particular crises? "My God," I cried dejectedly, "why can't my church help with the extra burden you have given my husband and me because we are so exceptional, so wise, so courageous?"

The best thing I did during the first year was to return to work. Although I didn't always feel like a good mother, I knew I was a good nurse. It took me away from Heather a bit and got me involved with others and their problems. It wasn't that Heather demanded much; her care was easy. It was the emotional stress which drained me, and working was therapeutic. I knew I was not being selfish, for I had to take care of myself in order to be a good mother.

I still find it difficult to sort out the spiritual dimensions of my ongoing experience. Anger and frustration with God and my church fluctuate with spiritual growth and increased reliance on God. The easy though well-intended assurances of friends and fellow Christians seem a facade covering fear of discussing Heather's retardation openly. This hollow comfort creates an unintended distance and makes it impossible for me to discuss the spiritual aspects and needs which are desperately important to me. In spite of the distance to which I, too, contribute, I urgently need to know that fellow Christians care about me, my husband, my child, and our ever-present hurt.

Pastoral initiative would be helpful. Support groups, such as Evangelical Concern's "Parents and Friends of the Handicapped," are necessary. Continuing assurance of financial help from the diaconate is important.

During times of obvious crisis, the support is supplied generously, but our child is with us twenty-four hours of every day. We, as parents, and our handicapped Heather never stop needing the concern, care, and compassion of our fellow Christians.

Heather is now two. She is recuperating well from recent heart surgery. She has become more joy to us than burden. She laughs more than she cries; she seldom complains. She teaches us patience daily and the meaning of unconditional love. We rejoice in her smallest accomplishments. She does not meet human standards, standards of intelligence, physical strength, independence. She does much more. She reaches God's standards: ". . . and what does the Lord require of you, but to do justly, and to love mercy, and to walk humbly with your God" (Micah 6:8).[7]

In this letter we see the pain in the working out of the death of dreams. It is important to remember that no one is ever prepared; it is always a painful surprise. As mentioned before, the family experiences all of the emotions of grief mature that are experienced when a loved one dies. The five stages of the grieving process are outlined below:

Denial and isolation

A sense of unreality
Unanswered questions
Fear
Mental and emotional
    blocking of reality
Inappropriate responses to
    inquiries by relatives or
    friends

Anger

Not easily verbalized
Must have a focus (e.g.,
    "It's your side of the
    family"; "It's all your
    fault"; "The doctor
    didn't . . .")

Ruins health
Ruptures relationships

Bargaining   "God, if you make my
                                   child well, I will . . ."
                                  "Doctor, you don't
                                   understand him; if I
                                   could explain you would
                                   change the diagnosis."

Depression   Longing for escape
                                  Apathy
                                  Feeling constantly tired
                                  Want to drop out of life
                                  Nothing matters
                                  No one cares

Acceptance   Hope for healing

These stages last varying lengths of time, may replace one another, or even overlap. They become subliminal shadows on the outskirts of consciousness as daily responsibilities are met. Parents may feel like acceptance is far away. Acceptance is found only in agreeing with God—about his Son, about the child, about personal circumstances. It is imperative for parents to remember that every child is prescribed by God, perfect for his purpose and pertinent to his plan (Ps. 139). Every disabled individual is a person of dignity and worth, has a soul with an eternal destiny, and is beloved by the sovereign God. Therefore, realizing that God does know and care, the parents can take the youngster as he or she is and learn to know the child as a unique self. It's hard. But with acceptance comes a God-given joy and release and an ability to comfort others.

As Amy Carmichael expressed in her poem:

In Acceptance Lieth Peace

He said, "I will forget the dying faces;
The empty places,
They shall be filled again.
O voices moaning deep within me, cease."
But vain the word; vain, vain:
Not in forgetting lieth peace.

He said, "I will crowd action upon action,
The strife of faction
Shall stir me and sustain;
O tears that drown the fire of manhood, cease."
But vain the word; vain, vain:
Not in endeavor lieth peace.

He said, "I will withdraw me and be quiet,
Why meddle in life's riot?
Shut be my door to pain.
Desire, thou dost befool me, thou shalt cease."
But vain the word; vain, vain:
Not in aloofness lieth peace.

He said, "I will submit; I am defeated.
God hath depleted
My life of its rich gain.
O futile murmurings, why will ye not cease?"
But vain the word; vain, vain:
Not in submission lieth peace.

He said, "I will accept the breaking sorrow
Which God tomorrow
Will to His son explain."
Then did the turmoil deep within him cease.
Not vain the word, not vain;
For in acceptance lieth peace.[8]

There are other stressful family situations: the diagnosis, the birth of another child, school age, cessation of public education, aging parents. The greatest threat to the family members is frustration as they deal with the sameness of each day's routine and boredom with that repetition. Other children and family friends are often quickly bored by the impaired child's inability to keep up. The family usually adapts to a soothing and familiar routine for the slower child—and yet that very routine can chafe. Many times marriages disintegrate and the joy of marriage is replaced by the despair of divorce. A common statistic that is quoted is that 82–90 percent of parents of handicapped children end their relationship in divorce.

Quite often the parents of handicapped people seem to be more "together" than a lot of other people you know. Always smiling and contained, they present a carefree and cheerful facade. But what is behind their masks? The following chart gives some important truths for the reader to remember.

Hard Truths about Families of the Disabled

General

The parents have a 24-hour-a-day job—not all youngsters sleep all night.

Fatigue can result in illness.

It's almost impossible to find an appropriate baby-sitter.

Neighbors, friends, and relatives feel awkward and tend to drop away.

A simple trip to the supermarket can be full of stares and whispers.

Other children can be cruel.

People are thoughtless.

Daily tasks must be done in addition to the care of the child.

There is a constant financial drain.

The family is usually excluded from neighborhood, community, and church activities.

People may not include the child.

The Marriage

Mother may sleep with the child in order to keep him quiet and then find that the child won't tolerate nocturnal separation.

Mates go through stages differently, and vent the anger on one another.

Both may suffer from fatigue.

No time together, alone.

No one willing to come in and release them for a weekend or vacation.

The health of the marriage depends on the mutual acceptance of both parents, and on their reinforcement of each other's roles.

Mothers

Feel guilty because of neglected home, other children, or husband.

Have tremendous physical expenditures.

Experience great emotional stress.

May spend most of their time with the disabled child.

Are left out of coffee klatches and luncheons.

Are constantly dealing with anxiety.

May become sick or even suicidal.

Fathers

May feel neglected.

May have to take a second job.

May be ashamed of the child and of their own feelings.

Seldom are included in the medical, therapeutic, or educational activities.

Often withdraw in silent pain.

The Siblings

The maladjustment of the siblings of a handicapped person can be four times that of others without a disabled brother or sister.

Often mirror the parental attitude toward the retarded child.

Are often not told the truth about the situation.

Feel guilty.

Feel jealous.

Are enlisted as little "parents" because they are normal.

Are often embarrassed by their handicapped sibling in front of their peers.

Can have fears that carry over to adulthood.

The Disabled Child

May grapple with the anguish of rejection in his own home.

May be overprotected and/or underdisciplined.

May be abused.

May be talked *at* instead of *with*.

Discovers that as he grows older and larger he is hugged less often and left at home more.

Desperately wants to be able to be himself.

Realizing the impact on the family and the struggles they will face, the pastor may use the following practical pointers to assist him in ministering to families who have a disabled member. Remember, it is not *if* the pastor will use this information, but *when* he will use it.

- Call at the hospital immediately. Your concerned presence says more than anything else.
- Offer to be a third party in meeting with medical people. Learn what decisions the parents are being asked to make: e.g., type of treatments to be used or possible institutionalization. (Ordinarily institutionalization is recommended at the time of birth only in extreme cases. Home living with the family will usually be recommended for at least the child's formative years.)
- Suggest guidelines on moral decisions, while realizing the final decision must be left to the parents.
- Listen, listen, listen to the hurting parents and the family.
- *Do not* say: "You must be very special parents." This implies the parents can cope better than "ordinary" parents.
- *Do not* say: "It is God's will." While this may be true from one perspective, it is not helpful.
- *Do not* feel you have to defend God. He is the sovereign Lord of all the universe.
- Learn all you can about the birth defect.
- Be prepared to refer the family to helping agencies.
- Be aware of the needs of all the family members. Be sensitive to their feelings and listen to their expressions of frustration, anxiety, and fear.

- Be aware of the child with invisible handicaps. Often the more closely approximating "normal" the child is, the harder it is for the child and the parents to reach a point of acceptance. Included in this area are children who are minimally retarded, experiencing sight or hearing loss, perceptually handicapped, hyperactive, or brain-damaged.
- Stay in telephone contact with the family if you cannot be with them in person.
- Be aware of the ongoing crises.
- Rejoice when a retarded child throws his arms around your neck after the morning service. He loves you! Many retarded and physically handicapped youngsters have special love for authority figures such as their leaders.
- Be alert for signs of emotional disturbance or deep bitterness in the physically handicapped.

Like all people, the handicapped have the need to love and be loved, to understand and be understood, and to live a productive life not only in the church but also in their own community. The pastor can lead the congregation in helping each handicapped person reach the potential God has given him or her. The following guidelines are presented to aid pastors in doing this in their churches.

Guidelines for Leaders

Pastor's Responsibility	Congregational Response
Share, with the family's permission, your knowledge of the family's burden.	• Proper information quells rumors • Motivation for prayer support

Build attitudes of acceptance, respect, and love by word and example.	• Base acceptance on inward qualities • Medical knowledge dispels fear • Sacrificial friendship is the norm not the exception
Encourage the congregation to offer practical help to the family.	• Baby-sitting by teens and adults • Respite care for parents • Advocates for disability needs • "Surrogate" grandparents for *all* children in the family
Work in positive ways to involve all members of the family in the life of the church.	• Christian education programming for *all* family members
Plan programs to sensitize the congregation to the physical needs of handicapped people and their families.	• Disability awareness workshops • Transportation availability through the congregation • Parent support group • Emergency medical prayer chain • Personal notes of encouragement
Reach out beyond the congregation to handicapped people in	• Publicize church-based sport and recreational camping program

the community.   • Develop estate planning
                            committee
                          • Provide legal assistance
                            through specialists in the
                            congregation

All members will at some time be faced with ministering to handicapped people and their families in their congregation. It is our hope that this material has helped you come to a better understanding of the needs of the handicapped and their families and will enable you to respond to the suffering of such persons with helpful Christian concern and wise spiritual guidance.

REFLECTIONS

Read this sample letter from the mother of a mentally handicapped individual. Answer it as a counseling letter, using all that you have learned through this book and referring specifically to Scripture in your response. Be sure you understand the condition that your correspondent is most probably in and use sensitivity as you think through and express your answer.

Dear Pastor (or Teacher):
   They say my child is retarded, but nobody will help me. The doctors don't tell me how much Joey will ever be able to do, and I can't take care of him all my life. They don't really seem to understand anyway.
   My husband has left me—he doesn't understand how much Joey needs me and he doesn't seem to care. I've tried to go to church, but the people stare and pity us.
   It doesn't seem fair. Why is God doing this to us? We've tried to be good people, but God must be punishing me. I don't know what I've done and certainly Joey doesn't know and never will have a happy life.

I just want to say that I am sorry for whatever I have done that God is punishing us like this. Won't you please help me?

Sincerely,
A Confused Mother

4

You Want Who . . . Me?

Understanding the Basis for Ministry

Motivation without implementation is like a car with a tank full of gas and a dead battery. Both motivation and a full gas tank are of little value if not utilized properly.

Emotionalism alone will never bring about lasting results. One has only to study different phases of contemporary history to see that pure emotionalism rises like a meteor only to burn out as it reenters the atmosphere of reality. Groups were enthusiastic and motivated to reach out to the disabled when 1981 was declared the Year of the Disabled. People took notice of the mentally and physically handicapped. People were interested in taking signing classes for the deaf. Greater awareness of disability issues led to ordinances being passed before local assemblies and city councils. Yet afterward people realized that compassion and enthusiasm were not the same; consequently, many slowly backed out of offering themselves for commitment to and with the disabled.

A strong philosophical basis will outlast human emotion. The philosophical basis is the anchor that keeps the boat of emotion on a steady and steadfast course; therefore, it is imperative that a biblical philosophy of ministry be carefully developed and nurtured, not just considered an option to be discussed at a later time.

The purpose of this chapter is to give a philosophical basis for implementing a ministry that will benefit both the disabled and the workers within the congregation. The great tragedy among many evangelical churches in America is that they may feel the emotional tug to involve themselves in a program without the proper background. Much can be accomplished when there are philosophical principles to assist that obedient spirit in structuring a ministry that will bring glory to God. It is imperative that everyone who works with the disabled understands the philosophy on the following pages and seeks to implement the concepts in a proper perspective to each other so that a balanced, Christ-centered ministry is accomplished.

Building People

It is crucial to understand at the start that the goal in ministering to the disabled is not to build a program, but rather to build people—both those who are members of our leadership team and those who are disabled. To do so we must focus on three areas: salvation, maturity in faith, and service.

Salvation

Jesus Christ died for all people, both able-bodied and disabled. His salvation is applicable to the human heart in its sinful condition, whether the human frame is whole or blemished. The gospel message is without sympathy for the sins of humans, whether disabled or not. Consequently, a biblically-based special ministries program must continually make a concerted effort to make certain of the personal salvation of every one of its participants. Though the methodology may have to be adapted for the mind of each person to understand, the concepts of sin, repentance, forgiveness, and salvation should remain the same. Willfully ignoring and disregarding the gracious salvation of Christ will not go unpunished. It is not a matter of whether the disabled can comprehend the truths of God's Word, but rather whether they will choose to accept them when they are presented in conjunction with the convicting work of the Spirit of God, through an acceptable medium and media.

Maturity in Faith

I believe that every Christian has a responsibility to become mature in faith. According to Hebrews 5, maturity is achieved by exercising the power of moral choices. This power of choice is resident within each of the disabled, and it is up to the body of Christ to see that guidance is given to make certain that they are equipped to make the proper choices when opportunities are presented. Such choices involve the decision either to yield to temptation or to resist temptation and choose to exercise spiritual giftedness for the glory of God.

Service

Because a person may be limited in body or mind does not necessarily mean he or she should be limited in service to Christ. I appreciate this statement made by a woman in New Hampshire: "I have seen retarded minds within good bodies, and I have seen good minds within retarded bodies, but I have never seen a retarded spirit in either." I believe that the body of Christ should allow the disabled to utilize their spiritual gifts so that the entire body of Christ may be matured to the honor and glory of our Lord. Let us not hinder that spirit of love and service to Christ, which is so often resident in the heart of the disabled believer.

Your church and ministry mind-set will emphasize either organization or organism as the following chart illustrates. When the church views itself as a living organism and strives to develop people over programs, their basis of operations is seen from a biblical perspective. Interest is developed by examining how the workers need to mature in spiritual growth. Out of that growth will come effective programming. At the same time, an organism must be organized to survive. Your ministry should seek a balance between these two emphases.

Organization or Organism

- Revolves around programs
- Designs programs and seeks people to fill position

- Focuses on structure
- Seeks people with skills or abilities

- Function follows form
- Organizational needs can outgrow leadership
- Looks for activity

- Revolves around people
- Develops people and allows programs to grow through individual vision

- Focuses on strategy
- Seeks people with character necessary to develop others

- Form follows function
- Structure flows from leadership resources
- Looks for individual growth

- Produces "driven" people
- Administrative focus
- Burns out leaders
- Goal: To build a program

- Produces "called" people
- Ministry focus
- Builds leaders
- Goal: To build people

The mind-set that is chosen will determine the philosophy that will be adopted in one's programming. So many churches develop a program to fill a need and find people to "fill the slots," thinking that this system will bring them success. But this only results in developing a "me-only" mentality, and as the following chart shows, the inevitable results are emotional and physical exhaustion.

An Individual Focus
leads to a "me-only" mentality
which centers on
I must . . .
Solve all problems
Keep everyone happy
Run everything
which leads to
Demands
or felt needs
which makes the
Goal be
To keep everyone happy
which causes the
Program
to respond to
the Tyranny of the Urgent
Plate spinning
Putting out fires
which causes
Frustration

which leads to
Fatigue/Burnout

A biblical perspective in this new endeavor is seen in the following chart.

A *Biblical Framework* will have
High view of God
Authority of the Word
Correct view of man
The purpose of the church
The priority of the family
Biblical leadership
which determines
the *Why* of *Needs*
which establishes
What the *Goals* will be
to develop
How the *Programs* will operate
(Complementation and Distinction)
to be followed by
Evaluation

As a result of greater growth and development of the worker or the student, changes will take place. There will be a refocusing of needs, a redefining of goals, and a refining of programming. But it will always lead back to a reaffirmation of the biblical framework needed for effective ministry with lasting results. This correlation is explained by the following chart.

The *Completed Ministry Cycle*
is built upon a
Biblical Framework
which determines the

Why of the *Needs*
which establishes
What the *Goals* will be
to develop
How the *Programs* will operate
to be followed by
Evaluation
which will
Reaffirm the *Biblical Framework*
and
Refocus on the *Why* of the *Needs*
and
Redefine what the *Goals* are
in order to
Refine and *Redevelop*
How the *Programs* will operate
and followed again by
Evaluation

Ministry will always undergo change. Will you?

Once a biblically-based philosophy of ministry has been developed, the worker is ready to begin to discover the proper programming that will meet the spiritual needs of the student. Programming without the proper philosophy will be ineffectual, and little or no growth will be seen in the lives of the students. In the next chapter, we will examine the specifics of programming.

R EFLECTIONS

1. Utilizing the insights you have gained so far, write out your personal philosophy of ministry. Be specific and include Scripture references to substantiate your points.

2. Now that you have developed your philosophy of ministry, what steps will you take to see that philosophy become a living reality in your congregation? Think through a step by step process and write it down.

5

WHO ARE THESE PEOPLE?

Tailoring a Ministry Program to the Individual

One of the greatest frustrations that the special ministries worker faces is the establishment of progress in spiritual development in the disabled student. Without some type of instrument for measuring development, teachers have no way of ascertaining whether their teaching methods are successful in advancing the spiritual maturity of their students.

Custom-designed programming is an essential part of any ministry to disabled individuals. Though there should be general teaching sessions for all, there should also be individually designed programs to maximize the potential of each student. To do this, the teacher must know the student in all areas that could significantly impact the student's spiritual maturity. This would include family background and schooling as well as personal information. One of the tools that can be utilized to the teacher's advantage is the Special Ministries Student Survey. An example can be found in the appendix.

Upon completion of such a survey, the needs of the disabled are brought into clearer focus, and an individualized educational program can be effectively utilized. As stated earlier, though the principles of effective Christian education are universal, the application of those principles can be uniquely individualized. An example of the Individualized Education Program can be found in the appendix.

God's Word teaches that children are to be raised in the discipline and instruction of the Lord. The Old Testament gives instruction to parents (Gen. 18:19; Deut. 4:9 and 6:6, 7; Ps. 78:5) and to the Jewish people in general (Deut. 31:11–13) to teach their children God's laws. The New Testament reaffirms the Old Testament concept that parents are to bring up their children in the instruction of the Lord (Eph. 6:4).

If the Old Testament teaches that it was both the parents' and the nation's obligation to train children, then who should have the primary responsibility? The family unit is ordained by God; therefore, according to Deuteronomy 6:6, 7, we can make the following assumptions:

- The primary responsibility for raising children should rest with the parents.
- The church should reinforce the teachings of Scripture and the parents.
- The Sunday school will assume greater responsibility for raising children from non-Christian homes; however, in such circumstances the priority of the church should be the salvation of the parents.

A Christian educator could have the following as a definition of Christian education: Evangelical Christian education is the Christ-centered, Bible-based, pupil-related process of communicating God's written Word through the power of the Holy Spirit, for the purpose of leading pupils to Christ and building them up in Christ.

Christian education is not simply applying secular teaching principles and methodologies within the framework of the church. Christian education goes beyond principles and techniques. There are three indispensable factors that make Christian education distinctive:

1. *The centrality of God's revelation.* To seek to have Christian education without the Word of God is to eliminate the basic core of the curriculum.
2. *The necessity of regeneration.* Unregenerate teachers cannot communicate Christian truths in the true sense of the word, since they do not know them experientially.
3. *The ministry of the Holy Spirit.* The Holy Spirit's work is necessary for spiritual enablement in every phase of teaching and learning.

Scripture defines the goal of Christian education as a "trained up" child (Eph. 6:4). The child needs to reach a level of maturity in which he or she is self-disciplined and acting on the foundation of God's Word.

All scripture is inspired by God and profitable for teaching, for reproof, for correction, and for training in righteousness, that the man of God may be complete, equipped for every good work.

2 Timothy 3:16, 17 RSV

The teaching process that results in maturity and godliness is Christian education.

In order to know how to evangelize or to edify disabled believers, we must know the individuals and their ability to comprehend spiritual truth. This knowledge will help us individualize our teaching techniques to best help them mature toward godliness. Even though biblical principles of godliness are universal in content, they are uniquely individualistic in application.

The Individualized Education Program and other forms in the appendix are designed to help workers become acquainted with the students. This gives the educators insight into each individual's spiritual aptitude. Notice that the Special Ministries Student Survey and the Individualized Education Program have universal application to all disabilities and that the survey is designed to seek answers to every area of the student's life—spiritual, social, and personal.

A cursory examination of the Individualized Education Program reveals that each division allows for three areas of personal development. It is important to match the development need with the process that is to be used (Development Need #1 with Process #1).

Finding the right person to initiate and follow through with a program to make certain that the process takes place is absolutely essential. Personal accountability is imperative because that is the only way an objective standard of development can be understood. Subjective thinking without concrete programming that utilizes an effective process is of little value. This nebulous thinking that only *believes* something is happening in the life of the disabled individual instead of actually *seeing* something being accomplished is the reason for many discouraged workers in this field. On the other hand, objective progress that can be observed is a wonderful source of motivation to continue on. Individualized programming is a great tool because it enables workers to see that effective ministering is taking place.

Having discovered the disabled student's needs, the teacher seeks to develop the most appropriate approach to bring spiritual development to the student. This will include understanding the process to be used and the type of programming that will bring development to fruition in the classroom setting.

Leona was a mentally retarded woman who, because of abuse, had developed great fears of darkness. Realizing this was a major problem that needed to be dealt with, her teacher designed the following program.

Development needs:	Mental, Spiritual
Process to be used:	Private discussion
	Individual teaching time
Program to be developed:	Walk with Leona in the dark
	Teach Bible verse
Person responsible:	Barbara

Realizing that Leona's need was mental (overcoming fear) and spiritual (realizing Jesus would be with her), Barbara was assigned to be responsible for helping Leona with this problem. Through private discussions and individual teaching times, Barbara would walk with Leona in the dark and teach her Bible verses about Jesus' love and care for her. This would assist Leona in overcoming her fear.

Just as we have made great advances in teaching children through means of Bible clubs, children's camps, Sunday school, and youth activities, so we must put forth the same effort in teaching the disabled the truths of God's Word. The next two chapters will provide a detailed explanation of the components in the Individualized Education Program.

1. How well do you know your students?

2. What is your greatest desire for your students? List names of individuals and your greatest desire for each.

3. How can you see your desires changed into effective growth patterns in your students?

6

THEY CAN'T LEARN . . . THEY'RE RETARDED!

Discovering How the Disabled Student Learns

For centuries society has assigned all types of demeaning and derogatory meanings to the term *retarded.* In the past, the very word *retarded* conjured up the picture of a sub-human person acting and behaving like a cross between a gorilla and a zombie. Screaming, yelling, foaming at the mouth, snatching children from their cribs, demon possession, and all types of diabolical actions have been attributed to the retarded. To stereotype all retarded individuals with attitudes that are archaic and unfounded is a blight upon those for whom Christ died. This stigmatization of the disabled should have no support from those within the body of Christ.

The Learning Process

To alleviate fear and counteract the mental images of the past, we must remember this fact: It is not that the mentally handicapped *cannot* learn, they are simply *slower* in learning. One mother said to me, "My son may be retarded but he isn't dumb." That statement says it all. The mentally handicapped have a wonderful ability to compensate for those areas in which they are deficient. We need to understand how the mentally handicapped individual learns and what stages are involved for effective learning to take place. Understanding these processes will help teachers to be more efficient in their teaching techniques and styles. The learning process for the student involves five stages:

1. *Set.* Learning starts with the set of all the stored information from past experiences. The goal of learning is a change in the set and in the behavior that results.
2. *Sensory Input.* The sensory receptors take in information that is relayed to the brain. Using more than one sense will increase the likelihood that the information will reach the brain.
3. *Integration.* The brain processes the information. (We cannot see this happen, but it is evidenced by the next step.)
4. *Output.* True learning should elicit a change in behavior.
5. *Feedback.* This is external recognition of changed behaviors. We try to promote desirable behaviors and discourage those that are inappropriate.

Set

While we cannot do anything to alter the student's initial set of information from past experiences, we can be aware of the general characteristics of his or her disabilities. As we begin to develop relationships with our students we will also become more aware of what they already know, and we can present information that will help them mature at a realistic rate.

Sensory Input

Individualization. Activities and lessons should be individualized to suit the abilities and interests of each participant. Through individualization, material can be presented at the proper level, and the most efficient sensory avenues can be employed. The interest level of the students should be stimulated to encourage attention. The Student Survey is a vital tool for establishing areas of need for personal growth and thereby creating a customized approach to stimulate the student to greater maturity.

Simplicity. Instructions should be simple and concise. Complex commands will be confusing.

Brevity. Activities should be geared to accommodate the short attention spans of the students. If proper activities and materials are used, a longer attention span will gradually be developed.

Multisensory Input. When instructing the disabled, the senses of sight, hearing, and touch should be used whenever possible.

Basic Components. Learning takes place in order from the simple to the complex. When a complex task or concept is to be presented, the task should be broken down into several basic components. Each component should be overlearned before proceeding to the next.

Examples. Concrete examples should be employed whenever possible. Learning should take place from the known (concrete) to the unknown (abstract).

Accuracy. Irreparable damage may result if material is presented improperly at the start. Improper responses must be corrected immediately.

Note: Too often teaching stops here, at the sensory input stage, rather than continuing through the next three steps.

Integration

Repetition. In order for the handicapped to learn, repetition must be used. For maximum retention (remembering) of a concept, overlearning should take place.

Practice. Distribute practice time over several weeks when difficult tasks or concepts are being presented.

Understanding. Material should be presented at a level the student can understand, employing the above principles.

Output

Application. The student should be asked to apply the concepts that are presented. For example, he or she might be required to make a decision, differentiate, compare, match, act out, or predict.

Transfer. Do not assume that the student will automatically transfer the application from Sunday school classroom to home or school. Teach the application in as many situations as possible.

Feedback

Success. Provide experiences in which success is possible. If the student is experiencing success, he or she will be more willing to try new experiences in the future.

Reinforcement. Reinforce correct responses and behavior immediately. Verbal praise is very important.

Consistency. Consistency is essential for effective teaching of the mentally handicapped. Each time a proper behavior or response is exhibited, the individual should be praised. Each time an improper behavior or response is given, the individual should be corrected.

Applying the Learning Process

This process of learning was vividly portrayed to me by my friend Robert, an elderly gentleman with Down's syndrome. For many years Robert has been involved in the sport and camping programs through our church. He always looks forward with great anticipation to camping, and outdoor living provides a unique atmosphere for teaching truths that may be difficult for the student to comprehend in a structured classroom setting. One of the most important concepts that we seek to instill in our students is that of courtesy. We were teaching the importance of the "magical" words, *please* and *thank you.* We stressed that the word *please* would gain great pleasure and help in difficult situations. Robert was all excited about this new concept. He was faithfully saying "please" in his requests and was properly responding with a "thank you" when someone would render assistance. He was progressing so well that week.

We had taken all of our students for ice cream as a time to exercise our teaching principles for the week, and to gain the feedback that we needed in order to possibly change our teaching technique. When it was Robert's turn to order his ice cream, he was so delighted, anticipating the first lick. I asked him what he wanted.

"Ice cream," he replied.

"Robert, what are the magical words we've been working on this week?"

He thought long and hard. Then the lights turned on and with a great big smile he replied, "Abracadabra!"

I could hardly contain my laughter and surprise. Even though the words may not be exact, the concept of politeness that he had learned was the goal for which we were striving. Teaching to change negative behavior and enforcing positive behavioral traits is one of the components necessary to make a vital and growing ministry.

One of the most practical biblical truths that we have taught in our church ministry teaching times is that of prayer. Over a period of weeks and through the use of the learning process concepts we strengthened our students' understanding of prayer.

During week one, using two cans with a string attached between them, we had the students talk and listen to each other *(multisensory input)*. We gave a Bible lesson on prayer, and the definition the students came up with was, "Prayer is talking with God" *(simplicity)*. This short devotional lasted only a few minutes as the director shared Bible verses on the topic *(brevity)*. During week two we continued to teach on prayer and brought the emphasis from Scriptures down to their personal needs *(individualization)*. Again we used the can concept, only this time we lengthened the string until the teacher was further away and around a corner *(repetition)*. In week three we allowed individual students to participate and practice this concept until they understood that prayer is talking to God whom they cannot see. Many students grasped the concept of prayer for the first time as we moved toward the application of biblical truth to human behavior *(integration* and *output)*. At the end of each class period, a time was given for prayer requests. The results were truly amazing.

Though retarded in mind, our students are certainly not retarded in spirit. Their fervency in prayer to God for others would put many to shame. Their compassion and interest in the needs and hurts of others sets an example few non-disabled believers follow today. *Feedback* is the reward for all of the effort and labor of love put into our teaching.

The illustration of the concept of prayer has certainly enhanced the prayers of our students. They readily make petitions to God for family, health, and friends. A calm confidence and assurance is part of their character as they realize that Jesus is a Friend who will take care of their burdens and concerns. It has been truly remarkable to behold.

Developing Lessons

We have just gone through a great deal of material that speaks to techniques in teaching that can be used to bring about results we would like to see. Now we will look at some practical ways to help students retain what they have learned.

Use Concrete Information

Someone has said:

> I hear and I forget;
> I see and I remember;
> I do and I understand.

The diagram below is the pyramid of learning. Note that as lessons become more concrete, we retain a greater percentage of the material presented.

Pyramid of Learning

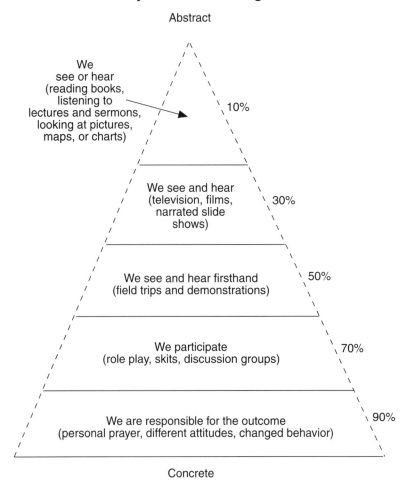

Abstract

We
see or hear
(reading books,
listening to
lectures and sermons,
looking at pictures,
maps, or charts)   10%

We see and hear
(television, films,   30%
narrated slide
shows)

We see and hear firsthand   50%
(field trips and demonstrations)

We participate   70%
(role play, skits, discussion groups)

We are responsible for the outcome   90%
(personal prayer, different attitudes, changed behavior)

Concrete

Understand the Levels of Learning

In his book, *Creative Bible Teaching,* Lawrence Richards
has identified five levels of learning. These levels are shown
on the chart below.[9]

Levels of Learning

Level 5

Life Application
Truth applied to one's life.
Example: Because Christ lived and died for me, I have been able to follow his example.

Level 4

Life Application
Relating God's principles to one's life.
Example: Because Christ lived as a man, he understands all my concerns.

Level 3

Understanding
Making application of biblical principles.
Example: Christ was born to live as an example and die as God/Man to take away our sins.

Level 2

Facts
Recognizing biblical concepts.
Example: Jesus was born in
   a. Galilee
   b. Jerusalem
   c. Bethlehem

Level 1

Facts
Repeating from memory.
Example: Jesus was born in Bethlehem.

As teachers, we must strive to bring our students to the level of realizing the application of biblical truth to their own lives. Richards expands on this goal, stating:

This is the goal of all Bible teaching: realizing, in the sense of making real in experience. Here is truth, applied in life. It's one thing to understand what response to God's Word is appropriate; to actually make that response is another.

Yet it's in the sense of "response made" that the Bible often uses the word *know*. In First Corinthians 6, Paul asks five times, "What, do you know . . . ?" In each case he asks this about a concept they had heard from him and were familiar with. He asks because their lives were out of harmony with the truth they heard. In the biblical sense they did not *know* these truths, for they were not living them.

This is the level of learning for which every Bible teacher vaguely hopes, but for which he must consciously teach. For, humanly speaking, learning that changes life is a product of a particular kind of teaching. Not teaching for rote to produce the ability to repeat without thought of meaning. Not teaching for recognition, the ability to recognize biblical ideas. Not even teaching for restatement, the ability to understand Bible content as part of a system. The Bible teacher must teach in such a way that his students understand the truth of God, can discover and are led to make an appropriate life-response to the God who speaks to them through His Word. Only thus learned can God's Word transform.[10]

REFLECTIONS

1. Think back on the valuable lessons that you have learned in your Christian education experience. What teaching techniques were utilized that caused the lessons to make such an impact on your life?

2. What would be some effective teaching techniques you could use in ministering to the lives of your students and their needs that you have discovered through the use of the Special Ministries Student Survey?

7

HELP! I CAN'T TEACH!

Developing a Curriculum

After the students' needs have been prayerfully considered, and the most effective process that can be used to meet those needs has been discovered, students with the same basic needs can be taught together. For example, if the Special Ministries Student Survey has shown that some students have a need to combat fear and to grow in their trust of Christ for security, a series of lessons could be developed that would center on this area of God's concern for his children. A unit plan could then be developed.

Unit Plans

A unit plan is a general overview of a multi-lesson topic. The unit approach to teaching the mentally handicapped is both functional and consistent with learning principles applicable to that population. When properly planned, unit teaching provides a sequential approach to instruction, and students are not subject to a hit-or-miss approach to their lessons. A well-constructed unit plan should contain the following elements:

Title. A descriptive heading for the unit.

Introduction. One paragraph to introduce the main subject of the unit.

Goals. The broad, general aims of the unit.

Content. A brief description of the lessons.

Evaluation. An inventory to determine whether the goals and behavioral objectives of the unit have been realized in the lives of the students.

Resources. A bibliography and list of resources used in the unit that function as supplementary information.

The following is a sample of a unit plan based on Psalm 23.

Unit Plan: Psalm 23

Title
The psalm can be entitled "David's Shepherd: The Lord."

Introduction
Psalm 23 is a familiar portion of Scripture; most Christians have heard it recited, but few realize the wealth of information found in those six verses.

Goals
  1. To understand that God wants to be our Good Shepherd.
  2. To understand that God wants to restore (fix) our souls.

3. To understand that God wants to give us many gifts that will cause our lives to overflow with goodness.
4. To understand that we will live forever with the Lord.

Content
1. Lessons
    a. The Lord Is My Shepherd
    b. He Restores My Soul
    c. My Cup Overflows
    d. I Will Dwell in the House of the Lord Forever
2. Assignments
    a. Discussion with family: Things that we fear.
    b. The "Goodness Shadow": Daily checklist of good things to be done at home.
3. Motivation Techniques
    The "Goodness Shadow" contract. Those fulfilling the requirements of their individualized contract will go on a field trip.
4. Special Teaching Tools
    a. Skits
    b. Demonstrations
    c. Puppet Show

Evaluation
1. The students will show improvement in one area of their home life for a period of two weeks by earning at least 75 percent of the total possible points on their "Goodness Shadow" contract.
2. The students will list at least one item that they fear and will pray about that item at least three times during the week for a two week period.
3. When asked the question, "Where do the Lord's children go when they die?" the student will respond, "To heaven with Jesus."

Resources
1. Phillip Keller, *A Shepherd Looks at Psalm 23* (Grand Rapids: Zondervan, 1975).
2. "Who Is My Shepherd?" Puppet Script (Share Time International, P.O. Box 5597, Buena Park, CA 90620).

Goals

Why have goals? The purpose of goals is to point us in a proper direction, to let us know how we are progressing, and to send us a signal of success when we have arrived. Psychologists tell us that we have a need to experience closure, that is, completion of a task. Satisfaction comes from pursuing and achieving a goal. If we do not set goals, we will not have the satisfaction of accomplishment. As the saying goes: Aim at nothing and you'll hit it every time.

The idea of setting goals raises several questions:

- How do we measure a student's understanding?
- Is "to appreciate God's love" a legitimate class goal?
- How can we measure the fruit of the Spirit?
- How can we measure a student's understanding of God's love?
- How can we evaluate our goals in view of the abstract nature of the concepts we desire to teach?

These questions are legitimate; to answer them, we must first look at how God causes change in the lives of his children. The concept that a change of behavior stems only from a change in the attitudes of the mind was basic to the message of the apostle Paul in Romans 12:2, "Do not be conformed to this world, but be transformed by the renewal of your mind, that you may prove what is the will of God, what is good and acceptable and perfect" (RSV).

Another important idea related to the formulation of goals is the distinction between a goal and an objective. The following definitions should clarify this distinction.

A *goal* is something for which we ultimately hope. It is not measurable in itself, but is a clear statement of the direction that we wish to move. Examples of goals include: (1) to have students manifest the fruit of the Spirit, and (2) to ground students in basic doctrines of the Christian faith.

An *objective* is a statement about a future event that can be defined, accomplished, and measured. It is a specific statement, not a broad generality, and it must be reasonably achieved in a way that is measurable in terms of time and performance. Examples of objectives include: (1) the students will exhibit patience by waiting for the teachers before each activity without complaining, and (2) the students will practice gentleness either by petting a dog or other animal with gentle strokes or by gently tapping the arm of a fellow classmate when he or she has done a good job of completing a class task.

Goals and objectives are tools that are meant to assist us in our teaching job by giving us direction. They are not meant to be tyrants to which we become enslaved.

Lesson Plans

A unit plan is broken down into smaller sections called lesson plans. The format of a lesson plan may vary from teacher to teacher, yet the items listed below should always be included in the plan.

Goal/Objective. To give direction to the lesson and stress major principles that should be retained.

Hook. To get the students' attention.

Foundation. To establish basic knowledge from which principles can be taught.

Instruction/Application. To make the lesson practical to the students' lives.

Evaluation. To measure the effectiveness of the lesson by the application of the principle into the students' lives.

In teaching Psalm 23, the *goal* would be to teach that God provides and protects. Objects could be brought into the classroom by the students to show what God has provided for them (food, pictures of home, friends, or others). This could be followed by having a policeman, fireman, or ambulance attendant come and tell how they help protect *(hook)*.

The teacher could then teach a series of lessons on how God protected people in the Bible, such as Daniel in the lions' den, the children of Israel, Paul in a shipwreck *(foundation)*. Time should then be allowed to help the students understand how God has protected them from trouble or danger. Maybe they can tell about a hospital experience they have had or a friend who was hurt. Even though we go through difficult times, God will be with us to help us *(instruction/application)*.

The effectiveness of the instruction may not be evidenced immediately, but at a time of crisis or need, the student's response to the situation will show the effectiveness of the presentation *(evaluation)*.

Curricular Materials

A curriculum is a course of study. Many publishers offer comprehensive curricula designed to lead the students through a course of biblical study spanning several years.

Recently, publishers have made available special education Sunday school curricula for the mentally handicapped.

Published curricula are intended to be an aid, not the answer. When used as a crutch, even the best curriculum can stifle the freedom and spontaneity that are so essential to creative Bible teaching. Curricula can also stifle the understanding we have gained through our own personal study of biblical truths, an understanding that the Holy Spirit can use in the lives of others. In general, a curriculum is best used to reinforce personal Bible study preparation. It should be used in conjunction with supplementary materials as a stimulus to trigger one's own creative ideas.

Because not every curriculum is perfectly suited to a class, one can rely on published material for a framework and then adapt it to one's own specific requirements. It is crucial for the teacher to know how to use published curricula effectively as a convenience and a help in meeting the special needs of the class. The following guidelines can be used in evaluating the quality and suitability of printed material that is available on the market.

Interpretation. The curriculum must feature a proper presentation and interpretation of God's Word.

Excellence. The curriculum should be prepared by scholarly and otherwise capable writers.

Framework. The curriculum must reflect the framework of Christian education as it is discussed in Deuteronomy 6.

Utility. The curriculum should be practical in the lives of the students.

Awareness. The curriculum must reflect an awareness of the factors that will hinder learning God's Word, that is, sin in the lives of students or teachers.

Commitment. The curriculum must stress the importance of committed, Spirit-filled teachers to the instruction process.

The simplicity of children's curricula makes it more easily adaptable for the special student than adult material. However, when adapting children's curricula for disabled adults, consider the following.

Pictures. Childish pictures may be demeaning to the mentally handicapped adult and may reinforce childish behavior. The pictures used should be simple in composition with a minimum of detail.

Abstractions. As children mature, they are progressively presented with more and more abstract concepts. The curriculum may need to be changed if the concepts are beyond the grasp of the students.

Vocabulary. If the vocabulary level in the material is too advanced, the students will lose interest. Non-reading lessons should be used since many students may not read and may learn best through manipulation of real objects.

Memory. Memory verses can be paraphrased and words can be replaced with pictures that illustrate the concept presented in the verse.

Music. Songs and words can be simplified, and hand motions can be included. Songs should be consistent with the thrust of the lesson to emphasize specific points.

Crafts. Craft projects may need to be altered or simplified to fit the abilities and interests of students.

Application. The truths taught in the lessons should be related to different real-life situations (school, home, or friends).

Stories. Keep stories short, picturesque, and realistic.

Discipline

Even though the disabled may have physical or mental limitations, that does not excuse them from accountability before God for their actions. Therefore, in order to have the greatest effectiveness in teaching, and in order for the teacher to be a good steward of the time that God has given him or her for the instruction of the students, it is imperative that there be good classroom management. The atmosphere should not be one of a concentration camp, but neither is it to be one of a circus. The teaching atmosphere is to be one where the students are stimulated to learn the greatest amount of truth in a limited amount of time. Truth that is simply knowledge-based is somewhat effective, but truth that has personal application is going to result in greater effectiveness for the students. That effectiveness will be seen in changed lives. In order to create the atmosphere that enhances this type of learning, discipline must be maintained in the classroom.

The English word *discipline* comes from the same root as the word *disciple,* i.e., a learner or follower. Because the child has not reached maturity, he or she needs direction, teaching, instruction, and a certain measure of compulsion and chastisement. The special services worker should equate discipline with guidance, not just with chastisement. The necessity for effective discipline is illustrated by the fact that the child's natural inclinations are directly contrary to God's principles of life.

There are three basic attitudes that demonstrate the need for discipline:

1. Disrespect of persons
2. Disobedience toward God and God-given authority
3. Patterns of irresponsibility in the face of known responsibilities

If these attitudes are not corrected at home, they will transfer to another sphere. For example, if a child is not corrected for being disrespectful at home, that attitude will prevail at school and in church.

Effective discipline is a two-phase process. The first phase involves communication and counseling, while the second phase involves the actual employment of disciplinary action.

Phase One: Communication and Counseling

To establish discipline, an effective channel of communication must be developed and maintained so that the person subject to the discipline is informed of the do's and don'ts. To do this properly, both the rules and the principles behind the rules must be communicated. An example of this kind of communication is shown in the rule, "We do not tease other students," along with the principle, "God wants us to love others; when we tease other students, we are not loving them."

The rules must be fair and consistent. The teacher must decide what behavior is acceptable and what behavior is not acceptable. Each time the child behaves in an unacceptable manner, he or she must be corrected.

A good counseling system is essential. The first time a child is disrespectful, disobedient, or irresponsible, the teacher should counsel that child. The purpose of counseling is to clarify and reemphasize the instructions. The teacher should consider the following questions during the counseling:

- Was my instruction clear? Did I provide enough information to correctly perform the task I gave him or her? Were the instructions understood?

- Was the child rebellious or merely immature? Was the disobedience the result of his or her being rebellious, or was I expecting more maturity than I should have?
- Is there a situation at home that may be precipitating this behavior? Is the child well cared for at home? Are the parents meeting his or her physical, emotional, mental, and spiritual needs?
- Will my warning appeal to the child's conscience? Is the child aware that he or she has displeased God?
- Was the child's behavior consistent with his or her personal goals? Have I helped the child set up personal goals? What goals are lacking in this child's life? How can I motivate him or her to internalize new goals?

When warning a child, the primary appeal should be to the conscience. Notice how the following statements differ in their primary appeal to the child.

Physical. If you tease Donald again you will not get refreshments.

Mind. Do you think that was a smart thing to do?

Conscience. Do you think that God would be happy with your teasing?

Will. Promise me you will not tease Donald again.

Emotions. You will really hurt me if you tease him again.

To appeal to the conscience of the child is to cooperate with the Spirit of God. It is measuring the child's behavior against God's standards, not the examples of his friends or parents.

Once a child has been counseled and a warning issued, the child's behavior should be monitored. If the child persists in improper behavior, the second phase of the discipline process should be employed. Failure to institute the second phase at this point will increase the likelihood of the child's wrong behavior being repeated. Additionally, the child may interpret the teacher's failure to follow through as lacking in honesty and credibility and maybe as the absence of love.

Phase Two: Discipline Employed

If improper behavior persists, the second phase of discipline must be employed. This involves the following ten steps:

1. *Cooling off.* This step is important so that the discipline is in love, not in rage. It may be wise for the teacher to leave the class for a few minutes (if another adult is present) in order to regain composure. This will enable the teacher to deal objectively with the situation.
2. *Confrontation.* The child should be taken out of the classroom or to a corner of the room where the rest of the class cannot see or hear the conversation. If the confrontation is done in front of other classmates, the child may be demoralized and wounded in spirit. The child needs to be concerned about the offense that has been committed rather than about his or her reputation.
3. *Explanation.* The student needs to clearly understand why discipline is taking place. He or she must understand that a rule was broken, and that this brings consequences. Emphasize that the student is loved and that is why discipline must take place (Heb. 12).
4. *Confession.* The child should verbally state why he or she is being disciplined. Prayer to God should take place with or without the teacher's presence.

5. *Application.* The severity of the punishment should be in direct proportion to the offense and should be felt as a negative consequence of wrong action. Spanking should not take place unless parental consent has been given.

6. *Restitution.* If others were offended, discuss the need to ask forgiveness and to reconcile. This step is important because the child must assume responsibility for his or her actions.

7. *Forgiveness.* Be sure the child understands that both you and God will forgive him or her. Ask if the child would like to pray for God's forgiveness.

8. *Love.* The student must be reassured that he or she is still loved. Often a hug or an arm around the shoulders will help to communicate this point. Be sure to restore all lost privileges at this time. If the student is not restored to full class membership at this time, he or she is being doubly punished. Remember, the child has already paid the penalty.

9. *Reinforcement.* Help the student to know how to behave appropriately by exemplifying appropriate behavior yourself. Show the student how to apply this behavior principle in many situations to make it a part of his or her life habits.

10. *Praise and Encouragement.* Verbal or tangible praise will help to stimulate good deeds and increase the likelihood of their recurring.

The special ministries worker will probably find that the steps listed above will be effective in helping to correct inappropriate classroom behavior.

Teaching Principles

Webster defines a *principle* as "a comprehensive and fundamental law, doctrine, or assumption." An example of a principle is: God wants us to be in submission to those having authority over us. Principles are important because they give us boundaries within which we conduct our lives. If our principles are developed from God's Word, we will have absolute standards; however, if our principles come from humanistic philosophy, our standards may change from generation to generation. Remember this little poem:

>Methods are many,
>   principles are few.
>Methods always change,
>   principles never do.

Use the worksheet on the next page to think through how to apply principles in making practical application of the items that are listed.

REFLECTIONS

1. You have been asked to develop a unit plan to teach to your students. As a result of the Student Survey, you have found that many of them are having a great problem with fear. How could you develop a unit plan in order to bring about effective change in the lives of these students?

2. Write the principle and an application for the items listed below.

Item	Principle	Application
A student will be like his or her teacher.	My example is crucial (Luke 6:40).	My poor attitude will influence and affect others, so my behavior must be above reproach.

The role of parents and the church in instructing children.

The purpose of Christian education.

The purpose of the gift of teaching.

The requirements for the Christian teacher.

The role of the Holy Spirit in the instruction process.

8

LORD, HERE AM I

Knowing Your Gifts

Effective ministry can never happen without effective teaching. The New Testament mentions teaching as one of the spiritual gifts (Rom. 12:7–9; 1 Cor. 12:28; Eph. 4:11). As with the other spiritual gifts, the gift of teaching is for the common good, and it must be properly nurtured. Being a good steward implies that the individual gifted to be a teacher should take opportunities to develop this gift. Additionally, he or she should observe outstanding teachers, study the process of learning, and set high goals so that the gift will be appropriated to the glory of God.

The Holy Spirit decides which gift or gifts each Christian will have (1 Cor. 12:11). Our responsibility lies in effectively using these gifts (Rom. 12:6–8). Although teaching is not by any means the only gift useful in a ministry to the mentally handicapped, it is an extremely important part of the work with these special people.

Giftedness for teaching can be determined by considering the following three steps:

1. *Experiment.* Try teaching in various capacities (be a substitute teacher, lead a small Bible study).
2. *Evaluate.* If God blesses the teaching, you might assume that you are gifted in that capacity.
3. *Enquire.* Ask the counsel of friends who know you well.

The teacher must enthusiastically present the lessons to the students. Enthusiasm will come from diligent study and vivid understanding of the subject matter. The implication is obvious: *The Christian teacher must be a student of God's Word.* The truths of God's Word should be taught and communicated through lives that exemplify the Word and exalt Christ. Paul exhorted Timothy in this way (1 Tim. 4:12). In order for the believer to live the lessons being taught, he or she must be Spirit-filled (Gal. 5:16). The gift of teaching is a supernatural, Spirit-endowed ability to expound the truth of God. The teacher can effectively impart spiritual truths so that the learners know how to apply that truth in their lives. Remember, the Bible says the teacher has many responsibilities (James 3:1; Matt. 5:19; 2 Tim. 2:15), and therefore this duty should not be entered into without prayerful consideration and total dependency on the Holy Spirit's leading. As God enables the special ministries worker to effectively present God's Word, he or she is in a cooperative effort with the Holy Spirit to see the divine mission accomplished.

The Holy Spirit has a distinct role in the instruction process: conviction and teaching (John 16:8, 13), indwelling and teaching (1 John 2:20, 27), illumination and teaching (John 1:9), wisdom and teaching (1 Cor. 2:13). As the worker depends on the Holy Spirit working through him or her, there can be a holy anticipation that God will accomplish great things in the life of the disabled individual.

It would be foolish to think that the effectiveness of any disability program is due to the correct philosophy, principles, and practices, without considering the most important element—the person who is committed to work with the disabled. Without the proper character and godliness being evidenced in the life of the special ministries worker, the program will slowly grind to a halt or will continue to go through the motions without significant meaning and effectiveness in the lives of all those involved in it, students and workers alike.

The Pattern of 1 Thessalonians 2

First Thessalonians 2 sets forth the pattern that needs to be evidenced in the life of the worker and gives a summation of how the scope of this ministry is fleshed out in the life of the individual. Paul sets forth the ingredients that are needed in four different areas. He finishes the chapter discussing the joy of personal ministry.

Person—Verses 3–4

In this section Paul describes the persons who will be effective in ministering within the context of special ministries. They are people of *integrity*. This integrity has been tested through the fires of suffering in order that the impurities of their individual lives would be withdrawn and the godliness of their character would be seen not only by

others but by God himself (3–4a). As a result of what God
has done in their lives to purify and strengthen them, God
has entrusted to them a great treasure—the Good News.
Paul continually realizes that God is examining his mo-
tives as to why he is doing his ministry. Integrity is absolutely essential and vital in effective Christian ministry
no matter to whom the person is ministering.

Principles—Verses 5–6

The integrity that Paul has just written about will be
evidenced in two different areas. First, Paul says that the
person of integrity will be *honest in speech*. His or her
words will be truthful. He says what he means; there is no
"hidden agenda." He or she realizes that God is weighing
the truthfulness of his words, that God will be his judge.

Paul also says that the effective worker in ministry will
be one who is a model of *humility in service*. The special
ministries worker works for God, not to be seen by others. He or she does this ministry for the sake of the kingdom, not to receive the accolades of others. Though this
work may be unseen, it will not go unrewarded. God
knows the faithfulness of the worker in the furtherance
of his work.

Practice—Verses 7–11

If workers with the disabled are people of integrity and
if they are people who practice the principles of honesty
in speech and humility in their service, God will use them
in his work with great effectiveness in changing lives and
in the furtherance of his kingdom.

The persons whom God uses model those proper personality traits and principles in the kind of lifestyle that

is pleasing to God. Paul says in verse 7 that the effective worker is one that is *helpful*. To illustrate what type of ministry practice the special ministries worker is to have, Paul gives the tenderest picture of care and protection—a nursing mother. Just as a nursing mother gives her very life for the welfare of her child, so too the special ministries worker gives his or her very life for the welfare of those served. Paul says that he imparted his very own soul because these people were so dear to him.

As the special ministries worker spends time and energy in behalf of those served, the walls are broken down and the students gain a greater and deeper place in the heart of the worker. The attitude changes from that of a person who *is* a problem to the person who happens to *have* a problem. In order for this process to take place, personal sacrifice will be experienced by the person who is involved in the life of a disabled individual. This is further confirmed by the words of Paul in verse 9 where he explains that effective ministry entails sacrifice day and night in order to see personal growth take place.

The words translated *labor* and *hardship* demonstrate the concept of fatigue and strenuous effort expended for noble causes. Ministry can be and often is tiring. However, in the midst of his efforts, Paul always paid close attention to his own personal life. The man or woman of God not only works diligently to see growth take place, but also experiences great discipline to be certain there are no areas of weakness or inconsistency in his or her own personal life (v. 10).

Paul's walk was one of personal devotion to God and blamelessness before others. Because these qualities were evident to all, he had the credibility to continually exhort, encourage, and implore people to be all that God desires them to be. The same is true in the life of the disability worker. If there is no personal righteousness, then one has no right to exhort others to such standards. Hypocrisy is seen easily by any person being ministered unto, whether disabled or able-bodied.

Purpose—Verse 12

Paul states that all of his efforts, both verbal and physical, are done so that the persons he ministers to will walk worthy of God and will mature and grow to be more like Christ. Truth presented without personal change will often lead to discouragement and a feeling of hopelessness on the part of the worker who has put forth the effort. The endless repetition of basic truths, the long discussions and talks about the sovereignty of God, the seeking to understand the mysterious working of God through suffering, are all done in order that the disabled individual will grow in greater godliness and walk in a manner worthy of God. Hard? Yes. Time consuming? Yes. Tedious? Sometimes. Worth it? Absolutely!

"Why bother?" you ask. Verses 19 and 20 give us the biblical reason for the existence of a ministry to the disabled in the church of our Lord Jesus Christ:

> For what is our hope or joy or crown of boasting before our Lord Jesus at his coming? Is it not you? For you are our glory and joy (RSV).

1. Have you been called to teach in this ministry?

2. In light of Ephesians 4:12–16, on what do you base your answer?

3. How can you be more effective in your teaching? Are there any hindrances? Any helps?

Appendix

Special Ministries Student Survey
Individualized Education Program
Emergency Medical Form
Release Forms

Special Ministries Student Survey

Using a student survey will enable the teacher to have a comprehensive picture of each student's ability to learn and the methods that are most conducive to his or her learning process. The Special Ministries Student Survey below gives a well-balanced view of the students and their capabilities. The medical section gives understanding and warning to the worker so that any interruption to the learning process is not viewed with surprise and thus upsetting to the student and teacher. The spiritual section gives an overview of the spiritual condition of the student and how he or she is progressing in his or her spiritual development. The personal section gives assistance to the teacher by helping to determine what method of instruction will assist the student's spiritual development. The social section is important because it relates spiritual truth to daily needs. If several students have a similar problem, then one Sunday per month could be given over to a small group Bible lesson on the individual social needs.

All of this material is useless unless it is developed into a plan of action for the students' development. Accountability and follow-up are essential so that the students' spiritual development is enhanced on a steady level and spiritual progress can be seen and enjoyed by all.

Date _____

Interviewer _____

Biographical Information

Name _____ M/F ____ Age ____

Address _____

City _____ State _____ Zip _____

Phone (___) _____ Disability _____

Medical Information

Seizures? Y/N Type: Petit Mal, Grand Mal (circle one)

Other type of seizure _____

How often? _____

Medication? Y/N What? _____ Dosage _____

How often? _____

Spiritual Information

Has the student received Christ as Savior? Y/N

On what do you base your opinion? _____

_____

_____

Does he/she evidence the fruit of the Spirit in his/her life?   Y/N

What strong personality traits do you you see evidenced in this student's life (love, happiness, contentment, frustration, anger, fear, etc.)? _____
_____

Has he/she been baptized? Y/N When? _____
Where? _____

What is his/her biggest spiritual need at this time (salvation, scriptural comprehension, obedience in baptism, Bible memorization, working on an individual area or problem, other)? _____
_____
_____

Personal Information

Is this person verbal? Y/N Does he/she use sign language? Y/N
Other? _____

Can he/she communicate with others? Y/N
How well? _____

At what grade level would you place this person's mental comprehension? _____

How can we increase the comprehension level of the student? _____

- Visual? Y/N (pictures, flannel graph, puppetry, drawing, nature picture books, painting)
- Audio? Y/N (teaching tapes or books, lecturing, one-to-one discipleship training)
- Other? _____
Explain your answer: _____

Social Information

Does he/she get along with the others in the class?   Y/N
How well? _____

Does he/she relate to peers?   Y/N
How well? _____

Does he/she respond to authority and commands by the leaders? Y/N
How well? _____

What is his/her greatest social need? _____

How can we as individuals or a ministry meet this need? _____

Individualized Education Program

The Individualized Education Program helps workers to tailor a program to an individual's needs. It allows for three areas of personal development and matches each development need to a process, program, and individual to be responsible for fulfilling the process. It is important to match the development need with the process that is to be used (Development Need #1 with Process #1).

Name of student _____ Age _____

Date of interview _____ Place _____

Interviewer _____

Phone ( ) _____

Development need: Social, Spiritual, Physical, Mental

1.

2.

3.

Process to be used: Private discussions, group lessons, individual teaching times
(Match process with need above)

1.

2.

3.

Program to be developed to fulfill the process:
(Deals with the content of presentation)
1.
2.
3.

Person/group responsible for fulfilling the process:
(Match person with the process)
1.
2.
3.

Emergency Medical Form

The Emergency Medical Form is a must for every student regardless of the disability. In case of an emergency, this form would give valuable information to the medical team that is aiding the person involved. Make your form as comprehensive as possible and also make certain that the insurance of the local church covers any transportation needs that the disabled may have in an emergency. This form should complement your student survey sheets in order to give a comprehensive picture of the students and the various needs that they deal with on a daily basis.

Name _____ Today's date _____

Birth date _____ Phone ( ) _____

Home address _____

City _____ State _____ Zip _____

Father's name _____

Address _____

Home phone ( ) _____ Business phone ( ) _____

Work days _____ Work hours _____

Business address _____

Mother's name _____
Address _____
City _____ State _____ Zip _____
Home phone ( ) _____ Business phone ( ) _____
Work days _____ Work hours _____
Business address _____

In an emergency, if parents cannot be reached, please notify:
Name _____ Phone ( ) _____
Relationship _____
Address _____
City _____ State _____ Zip _____

Physical handicap _____ Seizures? _____

Circle all that are appropriate:
Heart Condition   Lung Condition   Allergies
Stoma   Catheter   Shunt   Medication
Wheelchair   Crutches/Cane   Braces   Other

Comments and additional information: _____
_____

Release Forms

Medical Release

We, the undersigned parents or legal guardians of _____, a minor, do hereby authorize any adult person in whose care the said minor has been entrusted by _____ Church to consent to any X-ray examination, anesthetic, medical or surgical diagnosis or treatment, and hospital care to be rendered to said minor under the general or special supervision and upon the advice of a physician and surgeon licensed under the provisions of the Medicine Practice Act and to consent to an X-ray examination, anesthetic, dental, or surgical diagnosis or treatment, and hospital care to be rendered to said minor by a dentist licensed under the provisions of the Dental Practice Act.

It is understood that this authorization is given in advance of any specific diagnosis, treatment, or hospital care being required. The above authorization is given pursuant to the provisions of the Civil Code of this state.

Consent and Release from Liability

I desire to participate in activities of _____ Church. In consideration of _____ Church providing these activities, I do hereby release Church, its officers, employees, agents, and members of the Board of Elders from all claims and causes of action by reason of any injury which may be sustained as a result of these church activities, whether on the church premises or on the way to or from these activities.

Signature of parent or legal guardian _____

Date _____

I have read, understood, and agreed with the above statement as it applies to me.

Signature of participant (18 years or older) _____

Date _____

Personal physician's name _____

Address _____

City _____ Phone (___) _____

Name of accident/health insurance _____

Policy no. _____

Photographic Release

We also give _____ /do not give _____ (initial one) our consent to _____ Church to photograph the above named person and without limitation, to use such pictures and/or stories in connection with any work _____ of _____ Church and do _____ /do not _____ (initial one) hereby release _____ Church from any claims whatsoever which may arise with regard thereto.

NOTES

1. H. Oliver Ohsberg, *The Church and Persons with Handicaps* (Scottdale, Pa.: Herald Press, 1982), 69.

2. R. Kent Hughes, *Disciplines of a Godly Man* (Wheaton: Crossway Books, 1991).

3. Don Baker, *Pain's Hidden Purpose* (Portland: Multnomah Press, 1984), 14–15. Used by permission.

4. Ibid., 9–10. Used by permission.

5. George Peterson, *Helping Your Handicapped Child* (Minneapolis: Augsburg, 1975), 41. Used by permission.

6. Claudia Minden Weisz, "And God Said No," *Christian Parenting Today* (July/August 1989), 32.

7. Donna DeBoer. As told to L. V. Grissen, July 1977.

8. Quoted in Charles Swindoll, *Improving Your Serve* (Waco, Tex.: Word, 1990), 186–87. Used by permission of Christian Literature Crusade (for orginal source—Amy Carmichael's *Toward Jerusalem*).

9. Taken from Lawrence Richards, *Creative Bible Teaching* (Chicago: Moody Press, 1970), 187. Used by permission.

10. Ibid., 265.